Organization and Management in Schools

Perspectives for practising teachers and governors

SECOND EDITION

ALAN PAISEY

LONGMAN

LONDON AND NEW YORK

Longman Group UK Limited,
Longman House, Burnt Mill,
Harlow, Essex CM20 2JE, England
and Associated Companies throughout the world.

*Published in the United States of America
by Longman Publishing, New York*

First edition © Longman Group Limited 1981
Second edition © Longman Group UK Limited 1992

First published 1981
Second edition 1992

British Library Cataloguing-in-Publication Data

A catalogue record for this book is
available from the British Library

Library of Congress Cataloging-in-Publication Data
Paisey, Alan.
    Organization and management in schools : perspectives for
practising teachers and governors / Alan Paisey. – 2nd ed.
        p.   cm.
    Includes biliographical references and index.
    ISBN 0-582-08098-3 ✓
    1. School management and organization – Great Britain. I. Title.
LB2900.5.P35 1992
371.2'00941 – dc20   91-39869
                                                                   CIP

set by 9 in Erhardt

Printed in Malaysia by CL

Organization and Management in Schools

SECOND EDITION

Contents

Preface

Within a very short space of recent time the geo-political face of large parts of the world has changed on an unimagined and unanticipated scale. Within the United Kingdom itself life has been changing quite dramatically in many ways in the process of developing an identity in the European Community. Not least of these changes has been that which has taken place in the education system, including radically new funding arrangements, direction over the curriculum and modifications to the autonomy and powers of individual institutions. All these events have a bearing on the child or young person by way of what is taught or how it is taught by those responsible for the delivery of his or her education in schools.

Organization and management in the school are the means by which education is delivered. They are simply tools for this purpose and never an end in themselves. They are endlessly adjustable in the service of a fixed objective, the education of the particular child or young person enrolled in the school at the time. Organization is the set of human arrangements by which two or more persons work together; it can involve very large numbers of people, as in the case of schools. Management is that part of the total activity which is concerned with setting up organization and maintaining and modifying it to realize declared and explicit objectives.

The provision of necessary organization and management in schools is a complex task and the responsibility of the teaching staff themselves acting in conjunction with the governing bodies. This book is addressed to their interests. It offers perspectives on the central concerns of those involved in organization and management at all levels in schools. In organization and management studies and practice – as in education itself – fashions and particular interests and applications ebb and flow, but principles remain. Whilst this text cannot entirely escape the particular interests and applications of the date of its publication, it attempts to stay with principles to provide the reader with maximum scope for making applications in his or her own way to suit the inevitably unique set of conditions and circumstances within which organization and management have to be established at a particular point in time.

Chapter I explores a number of fundamental concepts together with an examination of the variety of views about them and values attached to them which may be found in a body of people involved in organization and management. Chapter 2 is focused on the very purpose for which organization and management exist with a special emphasis on the concept of objectives. Chapter 3 analyses the wide range of skills which are now needed to launch and sustain organization and management in schools. Chapter 4 is devoted to the concept of structure and considers the various shapes which organization may take. Chapter 5 on management style is concerned with obtaining results, without which nothing can be justified and the final chapter takes account of the fundamental importance of staffing in dealing with the subjects of staff performance and development.

Many friends and former colleagues in schools and other branches of the education service have contributed directly or indirectly to this book by their example of good practice and informative discussion. In particular thanks are due to Joyce Meadowcroft, Head of Four Lanes County Junior School, Basingstoke, Hampshire and to Jean Jefferson, Head of Sarum Westwood St Thomas Comprehensive School, Salisbury, Wiltshire. In addition, a special note of thanks is recorded to my wife, Audrey Paisey, whose substantial experience in teaching, teacher education and education management training has enabled her to offer critical observations and valuable suggestions in the writing of this book. Its remaining inadequacies are mine.

Alan Paisey
Salisbury, Wiltshire
1992

List of Figures

List of Tables

Acknowledgements

We are indebted to the following for permission to reproduce copyright material:
the author, B. Cooper for his letter to *The Daily Telegraph* 19 May 1979; the Controller of Her Majesty's Stationery Office for an abridged extract from DES, *Aspects of Secondary Education in England* (1979); Marshall Editions Limited for Figure 3.1 'Budget Cycle Model' from *The Managers's Handbook*; The Headmistress, the Sir John Cass's Foundation and Red Coat Church of England Secondary School for Table 2.2; McGraw-Hill Inc. for Table 2.3 'Importance of organizational objectives' from *The Management of Organizations* (1976) by H.G. Hicks and C.R. Gullett, © McGraw-Hill Inc. 1976.

To Mark and Timothy

1   *Thinking about schools as organizations*

Schools are not easy places to run. They are the scenes of potential controversy between conflicting interests in society which generate almost constant criticism of teachers. Schools consist of large numbers of young people whose views, habits and behaviour are very varied and may reflect a sample of the full range of interests and conduct found in the wider community. The teaching staff often hold differing views and expect to be able to have considerable autonomy on the basis of professional qualification and standing. Moreover, the concentration of such large numbers of people in relatively confined spaces tends to create psychological difficulties. The repercussions can be especially severe for the pupils as young people whose natural energy and adventurousness predispose them to physical movement rather than to long periods of confinement in rooms. In the past as in the present resources have never been lavish enough to be generous in the provision of space. The tight budgetary conditions which have generally prevailed for schools in the past have now been inherited by the school itself, under local financial management, charged with the prerogative and responsibility to ensure its own financial direction and viability. At the same time the objectives of the National Curriculum must be met as the nation through its central government tries to ensure common minimum standards of skills and knowledge among its children and young people.

In these and in other ways schools as organizations differ from what they were even a decade ago and are very different from what they were fifty years ago. It has become commonplace to speak of the rapid pace of change. More people than ever are prepared to accept changes or the need for constant adaptation as the norm rather than prolonged periods of stability. Yet in these circumstances there is a limiting factor. In ever-changing contemporary society, organizations probably develop faster than our ability to manage them. The management capacity is always being extended towards competence but never reaching omnicompetence.

The talent for good management is by definition in limited supply. There may be those who are born to it but if that is the case they are in short supply relative to the demand. The majority of people at work would seem to need systematic opportunities for the development of natural talent where it exists or the generation of it where it does not. This implies on-the-job monitoring of potential and exposure for growth plus off-the-job explicit education and training. In schools, as in all organizations, the resources which have to be managed, including time, are subject to alternative uses, making it difficult but necessary to achieve an optimum deployment and use of staff, accommodation, finance, materials and equipment alongside pupil grouping. Being a teacher involves a great deal more than being accomplished as an instructor and being able to enforce orderly behaviour. It requires a capacity for management. Such a capacity is a necessary part of the professional standing and qualification of the teacher. Without it, teachers may not only fall short of being able to manage the school successfully, but also suffer personal strain and perhaps failure.

All in all, to bring a school to the point of being a harmonious and purposeful unitary enterprise is a difficult feat of organization and management; achieving this is a professional accomplishment of the first order. It is known that all *kinds* of people can achieve such a result. It is partly science and partly an art, requiring politicial sensitivity. In setting out on such a task it can be said that the beginning of wisdom is to recognize that there is no single and irrefutable formula to be learned and applied. Knowledge of a general nature is involved, including the wide range of theories derived from the experience of others. Personal skills of many kinds are involved, including those which may be acquired by imitation or by deliberate study away from the job. In the end, however, management is a practical activity, undertaken for real purposes with real people. It has specific aspects, therefore, involving particular knowledge, singular personalities and local variations of principle, custom and purpose. There is always a unique flavour – though varied in strength – to the management of every school.

It may be asserted that there is no *one* way to manage a school, only that management is always partly subjective, partly objective; partly concerned with values, partly concerned with facts; partly a matter of intuition, partly a matter of measurement.

Definitions in education

There is justification for the fact that confusion reigns in the minds of many teachers over the concept of management. A number of different but related words and phrases are in widespread use. They are either ambiguous or seem to be similar to one another. Probably the most frequently used and the most ambiguous word in the teacher's vocabulary is that of 'education' itself. The term 'management' clearly brings further ambiguity to that vocabulary. The situation is compounded by the additional use of two phrases derived from these two words – 'management education' and 'education management'.

'Education' and 'management' are large and complex concepts. Many definitions of each may be found in the respective bodies of international literature available for students in these fields of study. It is clear that no single definition in either field commands the unreserved acceptance of all. It is necessary to reduce ambiguity as far as possible, however, even though precision cannot be achieved in such studies, which essentially lack the characteristics of exact sciences. Hence, for the practical purposes of writing this book a number of working definitions have been borne in mind. These are offered as an indication of the critical distinctions between education, management and the two important derivations which are in common use today. They provide a basis for thinking about the management of a school as an organization and the education of young people which schools are intended to provide.

EDUCATION
is the personal learning process by which values, attitudes, information and skills are acquired and integrated

MANAGEMENT EDUCATION
is the personal process of learning values, attitudes, information and skills to achieve desired relations between resources and objectives

---

In behavioural terms it may be seen from these definitions that 'education' and 'management education' are personal experiences which imply changes in the individual concerned. Other people may certainly be involved in various capacities to facilitate and promote such experiences. In the final analysis, however, the individual decides how receptive he or she will be to what is offered and what use is made of it. The element of personal choice and freedom is foremost.

MANAGEMENT
is the universal and unavoidable personal and organizational process of relating resources to objectives

EDUCATION MANAGEMENT
is the particular process of relating resources to objectives required in organizations which explicitly exist to provide education

---

In contrast, 'management' and 'education management' are inescapably concerned with *confining* freedom of action. These terms are for the selective behaviour and a limited interpretation of events in the service of particular objectives which affect all organization members, including those who formally occupy management positions. Both the organizational members and the physical or non-human resources which they command are intentionally devoted to the realization of specific outcomes. Certain behaviour is therefore legitimate in that it manifestly contributes to the desired ends. Other behaviour is not legitimate in that it does not contribute to the desired ends or it may actually prevent the organization from reaching them, or retard its progress towards them.

Confusion may arise in schools because in the act of being 'educated' one is also being 'managed'. In addition, the corollary applies. In the act of managing in organizations, one is hopefully learning and, therefore, undergoing an educational experience.

In schools and other educational institutions, the similarity of these concepts and their interrelatedness may easily lead to confusion. The critical distinction, however, must constantly be borne in mind. Managerial behaviour is directed towards the prescribed and limited use of human and non-human resources in order to achieve collectively explicit and desired results.

Failure to understand the differences between the concepts 'education' and 'management' may cause imbalances in organizations. In organizations generally, insufficient recognition of the 'education' process that should take place among members to accommodate the ups and downs of commercial and economic life may lead to mechanical and ineffective 'management'. In schools and other educational organizations, on the other hand, the lack of clear recognition and understanding of 'management' may create an unbusinesslike attitude and climate. Time spent in meetings, for example, may be grossly squandered whilst the opportunity is afforded for members to conduct 'academic' exercises and indulge in rhetoric which may be appropriate in the seminar or classroom discussion but lacks relevance to the effective despatch of business and the taking of decisions.

'Education' and 'management' can and should co-exist for the health of an organization. In schools they are both very much in evidence but the respective domains of each and the critical distinction between them need to be professionally understood and reflected in practice.

It is unfortunate, however, that some teachers say or imply that it is disreputable or inapplicable to regard the school as an organization which by definition must be managed. Such views are based on the belief that specific practices used in other kinds of organization cannot or should not be adopted in teaching. They contain the assumption that behind the practices and techniques to which exception is taken, lie values and attitudes which are somehow reprehensible and inimical to teaching and the interests of children and the education process. This is usually an unexamined assumption, however, which often does an injustice to the attitudes and practices of managers in manufacturing and commerce. The main reason for it seems to lie in the belief that management is non-human and that good management implies being devoid of concern for people. At the same time this assumption may be a convenient excuse in schools for not taking the kind of action needed to achieve effective organization. Such action may involve objective criteria that may *appear* to leave people out but which in reality are intended to safeguard and improve the lot of the organization's members.

The meaning of 'organization'

It is naturally expected that heads of schools and senior teachers are able to comprehend the school in its totality: it is in the nature of their jobs to do so. However, assistant teachers at all levels need to be encouraged to understand the school as an organization for three reasons. First, the individual teacher's work can be more constructively and effectively discharged if the whole to which he or she is contributing a part is fully known and understood. This is particularly important since the functional specialization to which teaching staff are often accustomed – teaching the same class or the single subject – can so easily be a handicap to an understanding of the organization as a whole. Secondly, it is characteristic of professional status to have an understanding of the whole and to take an active interest in the problems of the whole as well as the part. An increasing understanding of the whole school is certainly a necessary feature of the preparation for promotion. Thirdly, many heads and senior staff involve other staff in the management work of their schools and public pressures are exerted to increase such involvement.

In teaching, the term 'organization' has a variety of meanings. The individual teacher may speak of being 'well organized' when feeling on top of his or her work. This probably means that a programme of activities for every part of that teaching work has been thought through and prepared ahead of time. If this is actually achieved it relieves the teacher of the anxiety created when preparation is left to the last minute prior to implementation. If materials are made ready and a plan of action has been charted, the teacher is free to take care of contingencies, and to concentrate on assisting the pupils when the time comes to engage in the learning activity.

Similarly, teachers speak of a colleague as being well organized or disorganized, according to the degree of reliability on which they find they can depend. Teachers who are constantly weighed down and preoccupied with what is going to happen in their own classes are unlikely to be able to assist a colleague or share constructively in the wider activities and responsibilities which must be borne by the teaching staff of the school as a whole. A teacher must also be judged well organized in terms of how his or her pupils behave. Other teachers may readily perceive that the behaviour of a colleague's pupils and the level of their work are of an acceptable standard as a result of adequate preparation and leadership.

In addition, organization is also used to refer to the way in which the tangible objects in a school and classroom are used. The term is often used with regard to the functions given to certain rooms, areas, corridors and surfaces, the location of equipment, storage facilities and resources and the frequency, extent, quality and visual appeal of exhibitions of materials and work. A well-organized classroom can mean that the furniture, fittings, equipment and materials – in short all the *physical* objects – are arranged in the best order for the work in hand. The criterion for judging this may contain considerations of safety, ease of access, speed, quietness and availability for sharing scarce items among many pupils.

These uses of the word organization in teaching stem from the use of the verb 'to organize'. Thus, the classroom's physical objects and consumable resources need to be organized in the same sense that teachers think that they must be ready to organize the pupils. Equally, teachers may think that they should organize their colleagues, from time to time and for various reasons, if agreed activities are to be successful.

Organization as a noun needs to have a specific and restricted meaning. Hence, a number of preliminary points may be made about the identity and nature of organization when used in relation to management. In the first place, organizations are not things but people. The organization is the people who inhabit the institution. They have come together on the basis of declared interests and purposes which they find reasonably compatible.

The use made of buildings, materials, equipment and money depends on human intervention. Thus the lay-out of the classroom which earns the favourable or unfavourable comments of visitors to the school is merely a physical arrangement. Behind the state of the classroom, however, lie the thought and action of the teacher and the behavioural procedures which have been inculcated in the pupils. Behind these lie the thought and action of other staff and those in senior positions in the school.

In thinking of organization in this way it is plain that organization is a pervasive human phenomenon. Everywhere people get together to tackle difficult undertakings. Throughout the world of manufacturing and commerce, welfare and security services, sport and leisure pursuits, people organize themselves to produce goods and services.

> Organizations are people, not things

The question of which people in a school make up the organization, howeve., is a difficult one. The size of the school in part determines the size of the organizational membership, but the nature of the composition is open to different interpretations in different schools. The teaching staff are clearly accepted as the most eligible, less so the non-teaching staff. With their change of status and responsibility, the governors must be regarded as an integral part of the organization more so now than ever before. The pupils are thought of as members in some schools, but not in others. Visitors and auxiliary helpers such as parents are probably seldom regarded as members. It is never easy to draw the boundary line around the organizational membership. Even if tangible criteria are used such as 'place of work', 'source of remuneration' or 'nature of appointment', there is still the intangible or psychological criterion concerned with how people *feel* about the organization. On the latter basis, some people who have no tangible grounds for being counted as members may well be *regarded* as such on psychological grounds. Similarly, those who are paid members of staff, for example, may *feel* alienated and non-members.

The management of a particular organization must take into account *all the behaviour* which characterizes the group of people concerned. This includes behaviour which is wanted and that which is incidental or unexpected. Organization consists of 'networks of relationships' between people acting and reacting on each other, sometimes in accordance with intended ways of furthering the purpose of the organization; sometimes in ways which are intended, though not in terms of the official purpose; and sometimes in ways not intended by anyone (Emmet 1967:184).

Behavioural transactions *between* people in the course of their work form the most obvious example. Less obvious is the behaviour directed towards inanimate objects, as when working with machines or on materials for productive purposes. Least obvious but of great importance is behaviour which is not transmitted to others or directed towards objects but may be interpreted by others as signs or symptoms of the individual's physical and psychological condition as a member of the organization. This may vary from behaviour which can be interpreted as evidence of contentment and absorption in the job to that which is evidence of stress and incipient breakdown.

Although organization may be said to exist, therefore, when there are people with an ability to communicate, a willingness to contribute and who have aims and purposes in common (Barnard 1964), the human behaviour of which organization consists should be seen to include both *rational and non-rational* elements. In the early part of this century it was sometimes assumed that the concept of organization could be confined to what was rational (Taylor 1947). People might then be too readily regarded as passive, and subject to similar laws and predictability as physical objects. Taking such a position about organization members assumes that what may be planned may be implemented, since if people fail to cooperate with that plan, ways and means can be found to produce the necessary cooperation (Etzioni 1961; 1964). At the opposite extreme, the concept of organization in recent times has been enlarged to admit the non-rational side of human conduct (Hughes 1976; Greenfield 1977), particularly so in the case of schools (Turner 1977).

Members of an organization may not share a real enthusiasm for its objectives and interests and may even go so far as to sabotage its very existence. Clearly the self-interest of members, especially in some kinds of organizations, cannot be expected to be coterminous with the interests of the organization as a whole. Equally clearly, however, it can be seen that the balance between self-interest and organizational interest must always be in favour of the latter since organization by definition is an expression of *common* interest. In practical terms in teaching, this implies finding 'a single and coherent strategy both to enhance the personal and professional resources of the teacher and at the same time increase the school's capability with respect to change' (Light 1973:5).

From the standpoint of the interests of the organization, individuals are capable of exhibiting both rational and non-rational behaviour. They seldom confine their behaviour to one kind or the other alone. This evidently arises because in the transactions which take place between the organization and its environment, and between members of the organization itself, both matters of fact and matters of value are at stake. Facts and values respectively mean different things to different people. What one person sees as incontrovertible 'fact', another person may see as a value judgement. Furthermore, even when 'facts' are apparently self-evident, the interpretation or meaning which people place on them varies so much because of the different value-systems which individuals cherish. The view taken as to what is rational and what is non-rational is often held to be subjective. Nevertheless, it is argued that there is an inherent logic in every situation in organizational life (Howells 1972) which can be understood by every member. Thus, given the purposive nature of organization in the first place it seems both sensible and justifiable to take the view that 'most behaviour in organizations is intendedly rational behaviour' (quoted by Dunsire 1979:116).

> Organization contains both rational and non-rational behaviour

Organization as means to an end

It follows from the definition of organization as people that organization is transitory in nature. The actual number and identity of the people who make up the membership of an organization are subject to change. Any individuals who remain members for a long time are subject to change. The performance of an individual varies in response to the different internal and external circumstances which arise in the course of time in the institution concerned.

> Organization is transitory in nature

The varying group of people who comprise the membership of the school as an organization is limited but never isolated. Every organization establishes relationships with other organizations for many purposes. A study of the school as an organization must focus not only on its internal aspect but also on its *external* aspect, which is the way that the organization as a whole relates to and interacts with other organizations. The latter are themselves constantly changing and so provide an inescapable, and sometimes turbulent, environment. For any school, other organizations include other schools, economic organizations, pressure groups, the local education authority and many others.

> Every organization relates to many other organizations which form a changing and sometimes turbulent environment for it

A school needs and seeks a measure of stability. Excessive instability is regarded as a pathological condition to be avoided. The degree of stability which a school may achieve depends partly on internal factors and partly on the degree of instability of each of the other organizations to which it can choose – or is obliged – to relate. It is difficult if not impossible for the school to escape or even to influence the power of some of these organizations, notably that of the local education authority, unless it has exercised the right to opt out of its control. Others, however, may be avoided at will in order to safeguard or increase the school's stability; yet others may be deliberately cultivated. In the following example, a school has been subject to a degree of dislocation not of its choosing, but finds a way of redressing the balance, and in this case reducing the turbulent effects of the action of other bodies.

> ... school is not suitable to be used as a polling station, say town council-lors ... the most important thing [is] to move the polling station from the school. 'The idea of closing down schools so that politicians can come in is monstrous. Let's get polling stations out of the schools'. ... The committee recommended that the council should write to the district council urging them to use Trinity Hall as the south ward polling station, and not to use schools as polling stations during term time (*The Henley Standard* 1979)

As an organization the school is subject to constant adjustment. The reason for this is that the capacities of the staff who teach and organize successive generations of pupils entering the school each year vary in response to all kinds of constraints and demands levelled at the school from other bodies of one kind and another. Sometimes, however, the internal factors are greater than the external factors as causes of adjustment. This was very often true in the 1950s, the 1960s and the early 1970s when a shortage of teachers, high teacher turnover rates and burgeoning numbers of pupils in overcrowded buildings were characteristic of schools.

In more recent times, external factors such as financial constraints, parental demands and community expectations form the larger cause, in the face of falling numbers of pupils, and an adequate supply of teachers. The school does not have to yield to every demand made upon it – it would be impossible to accommodate every demand, anyway, since many are mutually contradictory. Nevertheless, it must be seen as a workplace which survives by constant adjustment to both internal and external factors. The organization is transitory in nature because of changes *of* members or changes *in* members, and because of the demands made of them or constraints imposed on them by other organizations. In the case of the latter, however, it has been shown that all kinds of organizations have various ways of moderating them (Gouldner 1955). Bureaucratic controls have been found to be frustrated in schools by teachers who used the pressures of the classroom as a counter-measure (Pellegrin 1976: 359–64). Most factors which relate to 'success' as a school may be regarded as open to modification by the teaching staff rather than fixed by external constraints (Rutter *et al.* 1979). That is, the school has enough freedom of action to become effective as an organization or to fail by its own lack of initiative and ability.

The work of the head and senior staff of a school is to accommodate internal and external variables as part of the management function. The better the understanding of developments which all the teaching staff can achieve, however, the more likely it is that the school will be an effective organization. The awareness of this point was shown succinctly by a postgraduate student-teacher on evaluating the first teaching practice: '. . . by studying the administration of a school, one becomes aware of the complexity of the whole organization, and how highly sensitive it is to different pressures'.

It is right that a school should be sensitive to the many different pressures which make themselves felt, not least because it does not for the most part originate its own resources. The work that it does must be subject to scrutiny and definition by many interest groups, simply because the products of all legal, social and economic organizations are for the use of others and are influenced by demand. The school is not an end in itself, like a private sports club or debating society, even though many of the activities and experiences which pupils have in them may be conceived in that way. The school is not alone in this but in common with all organizations must be accountable to its clients. Organizations, therefore, are essentially *instrumental* in nature, or, as defined tersely by Riggs (1957), 'organizations are agents'. In modern industrial societies they are agents for the control of scarce resources which are needed to produce and distribute valued goods and services. The purposes which organizations serve ebb and flow themselves and this accentuates the transitory nature of organization. Consequently, constant adaptation is necessary (Schon 1971). These purposes may be mundane and material or elevated and concerned with meaning. They are all related to human needs. 'A planned organization . . . is capable of transforming the value-content of institutions into tangible assets with great economy in the consumption of society's limited resources and efficiency in the use of manpower' (Popper 1967:70).

> Organization exists for the pursuit of declared objectives – it is instrumental in nature

Organizations in general are the means by which income and status are allocated. In the case of schools this is not only true of the teaching and non-teaching staff but also of many other occupations – such as in local government, the civil service and other educational institutions and agencies – which depend upon the existence of schools for their own employment. Even more important than this is the fact that schools as organizations affect the distribution of life chances and subsequent power of the pupils who pass through them.

The school has a delicate responsibility to respond to the claims being made of it and yet to act as a moderating and reconciling force. Many interests outside the school are reaching into the organization to influence the experiences, knowledge, values and sense of direction which are being imparted to the pupils. At the same time the school as an organization is reaching out to others who have legitimate claims to exercise such influences.

School as a workplace

As a day-to-day workplace the school consists of a large number of people – teaching staff, non-teaching staff, pupils and others, notably governors, parents and student teachers who are not on the payroll but who contribute to the work of the school. They are all variously working in large or small groups or alone. In primary schools it is the common mode for pupils to be in classes, each with an assigned teacher who designs and delivers the entire teaching–learning programme for that class or certainly the greater part of it. The demands of the National Curriculum mean that in most primary schools this is accomplished in collaboration with other teachers to ensure adequate curricular content, coherence, progression and effective coordination throughout the school. In contrast, in very small rural schools with, for example, only two teaching staff, the burden may fall entirely on the teacher alone but is increasingly likely to result from liaisons with colleagues who are similarly placed in other small schools in the region. In all cases, information, guidance and training may be organized and offered to teaching staff from time to time or on a regular basis to support them in this responsibility.

The primary school class teacher supervises the progress of the members of the class. Any of a large range of teaching methods, which variously involve the teacher and the pupils, may be adopted. The choice depends upon the kind of work being undertaken and the interests, capabilities and needs of the pupils as well as the skills and experience of the teacher.

Many reasons are advanced to justify class teaching. Among the most important is the child's need for a measure of social security and emotional stability. The teacher is enabled to understand the personality and interests of each child. The child is exposed to the values and standards of one teacher only, corresponding to the idea in classical organization theory that it is best for an individual to report to only one person.

In the case of team teaching, the responsibility for providing the programme devolves on two or more teachers acting conjointly with respect to a correspondingly larger group of pupils than a class. Planning, teaching and other duties are shared, and the pupils become familiar with different values and standards as they learn to work with different members of the team, rather than exclusively with a class teacher. Numerous advantages have been identified for this way of teaching (e.g. Forward 1971). One of the most important benefits is that of enabling the pupil to get used to working in a more complex organization.

In secondary schools the dominant feature is that pupils meet many teachers in the course of a week's work. Many variations of teaching methods and practices exist in both secondary and primary schools but the predominant mode is for each teacher to offer a limited, specialized contribution to the pupil's programme. By definition, teacher and pupil are less well known to, and understood by, each other than in the primary school. The pupil is exposed to many different and sometimes contradictory values and standards. There is a recognition of the growing physical and emotional independence of the young person, as well as the differentiation of their abilities and occupational destinations.

Whatever the kind of school and the particular modes which are adopted by teachers and pupils for working together, it is seldom that they will work in isolation for very long. Schools have become the place of work almost daily for a succession of other people who enter them for a variety of purposes. They may be classed as either 'official' visitors or 'unofficial' visitors.

Among official visitors to the school are Her Majesty's Inspectorate, who monitor all dimensions of the education service. They have right of entry for a wide variety of purposes, though actual visits in the case of a particular school are generally infrequent. Contacts are conducted in a cordial, informal manner and are usually free from the kind of forbidding relationships which the term 'Inspectorate' suggests (Department of Education and Science 1970). The local education authority (LEA) has right of entry for regulatory purposes through its education officers, inspectors and advisers, and where applicable for maintenance purposes through its staff who are responsible for architecture, building, heating, lighting and other services, the supply of educational consumer goods, furniture and equipment, and deliveries and collections in connection with the school's catering facilities.

A further category consists of personnel in various social services which have a legal or quasi-legal interest in the health and welfare of children. Numbered among them are the medical and dental services, psychological services, the police, the probation service and a variety of officers concerned with the care and condition of children in families. Finally, other educational institutions expect – and are normally granted – right of access. Staff from similar schools often frequent or are invited to visit a school for purposes of professional study. For example, liaison staff from infant or first schools may exchange visits with their colleagues from the junior or middle schools to which they relate. Similarly, this may happen between junior or middle schools and related secondary schools, and between the latter and related upper schools or further education colleges. In addition, as is commonly the case, if a school has agreed to offer opportunities for field experience to student-teachers as part of initial teacher-education programmes, it will then grant right of access to the staff of the higher education institution who are involved in tutorial and supervisory duties in respect of the student-teacher.

Unofficial visitors fall into three main categories. Foremost are the parents who wish to speak with the head or other staff or who have been invited to discuss matters concerning their children. A second category includes people who call for exceptional or intermittent purposes, such as to undertake research, to lodge complaints or to offer materials and facilities for the use of the school. The third consists of commercial representatives, visiting by invitation or on a speculative basis. Direct contact between publishers and manufacturers and schools is on a restricted scale. The sheer volume of lines is so great that LEAs have developed central buying and distribution facilities. Commercial firms and other bodies, however, may still keep schools informed of their products and services by mail and make visits to schools to give demonstrations and advice. Under local financial management, schools are able to exercise more freedom to make direct commercial contacts and contracts than under the previous financial regime. Under the opting out scheme provided by the Education Reform Act of 1988, a school needs to become self-sufficient in such contacts and contracts.

Pupils and teachers leave the school premises during the working day for many approved purposes. External activities of great variety and substantial curricular value have been regarded and still are regarded as a legitimate part of the curriculum for pupils and young people of all ages. But time spent out of school is now less willingly afforded. Some schools have even formally cancelled external visits. In pursuit of National Curriculum targets time is viewed differently and many schools have sought to extend their working day.

A special group of people who may be found in schools during the working day is the governors. The greatly extended powers and duties which they have to exercise in the 1990s and beyond require more time spent in the school and a closer involvement in its day-to-day workings. The governors may be regarded as neither official nor unofficial visitors but as an integral part of the organization and management of the school, forming its policy-making body rather like the board of directors of a limited company. Its members number from eight to eighteen according to the size of school, plus the head if he or she chooses to be a member – a legal right usually exercised in favour of membership. There are governors to represent the teaching staff – the teacher governors – and parent governors who are formally elected to office by the parents as a whole. Other governors represent the local education authority and a variety of other public interests, including industry and commerce. Some members other than the teacher governors may spend considerable time in school apart from meetings to give practical help and for observational purposes. One governor, newly appointed under the terms of the Education Reform Act of 1988, has described his task as follows:

> . . . my school governor duties keep me extremely busy. Governors now
> have the responsibility for hiring and firing teachers and paying their
> salaries, amongst many other things. I don't go to most of the training
> meetings offered for governors these days but I do feel obliged to attend
> more meetings now than I did at first. The mountains of paper we have

been getting from the Department of Education and Science and the local education authority could take up all my free time if I had not had previous experience of that sort of thing before in my own profession. Our local education authority has now decided it has vastly overspent in recent years so the pressure is on us governors to reduce spending in the school more than ever.

As a workplace the school is now more regulated by national legislation than ever before. A series of Acts of Parliament culminating in the Education Reform Act of 1988 has greatly altered the framework of discretionary powers, responsibilities and liabilities within which the school must operate. It follows that the school as an organization requires management which needs to cope with a number of important character-istics. Each of these is not unique but as a group they give the school its distinctive form as an organization. A school requires high initial capital outlay for buildings which may not have received subsequent commensur-ate maintenance and improvement to modern standards. It is labour intensive and therefore high in running costs with few, if any, oppor-tunities for automation to reduce them. At the product end it is difficult to simplify and rationalize production since the clients as pupils constantly change and the learning content to which they are exposed is subject to frequent modification and updating.

The density of persons per square metre of floorspace is high, making for high supervision costs and substantial losses of job satisfaction and productivity with rising job dissatisfaction through human friction. The proportion of administrative to executive (teaching) staff is very low. The volume of administrative work is in the process of increasing as the National Curriculum and local financial management together with other reforms move slowly through to full implementation during the 1990s, whilst teaching time retains the same share of the working week.

The National Curriculum provides specified production targets for schools for the first time which, together with staff appraisal procedures, represent a serious effort to operate quality control within a nationwide framework. This constitutes a basis for making intra-school and inter-school comparisons for shedding light on staff competencies, financial efficiency and the overall effectiveness of organization and management, given the number and calibre of the particular pupil body enrolled. At the same time staff are subject to being able to meet uniformly high entry qualifications for teaching and are eligible for unprecedented in-service training and developmental opportunities in the face of increased demands on their time and skill.

A school's budget and its financial management are notable for the fact that the bulk of disposable income is determined and provided by agencies outside of the school itself, rather than from the satisfaction, support and consumption of the consumers of the school's services and output. This is true for schools in the *public sector*, so-called because their funds are supplied by national and local government, the former bearing the greater part. The reverse is true of schools in the so-called *independent sector* which must raise all their finance from fees, alumni sources, gifts, subscriptions and bequests. Under the terms of the Education Reform Act of 1988, schools which have depended on national and local government finance may opt out of dependence on the latter in favour of being wholly funded by national government. The significance of this is political as well as financial. Local government as agent for the supply of public funds has been able to exercise strong *de jure* and *de facto* controls over schools in the public sector. In opting for national funding only, a school is able to assume even greater independence than is afforded under local financial management. In choosing to opt out a school must weigh the advantages and disadvantages of having the local education authority connection. For many schools this may seem like tutelage but may carry with it valuable services.

Internally generated income is possible in schools but is usually low in relation to the total official funding. However, the smaller the school the more likely it is that it will assume a higher relative proportion of total income. The scope for internally generated income is subject to much exploration.

The financial management of the school is in the hands of the governors with the head as chief executive. Their legal responsibilities are exercised on a custodial basis as public overseers of public expenditure rather than as directors with a personal financial stake in the enterprise. Profit and capital accumulation are in practice low but potentially, and in theory, local financial management and the right to opt out of local education authority control offer opportunities to make savings and to build up reserves.

Schools can be and probably are for the most part exciting if exacting places to work in. There is constant stimulation and usually opportunity – if not active encouragement – for experiment and creative departures from the norm. Above all there is the constant exuberance of youthful minds and bodies responding to rich opportunities for growth and development. The sheer joy of witnessing a pupil's learning progress can commonly be for most teachers one of the most unalloyed experiences of life and is almost certainly the biggest single element of the job satisfaction level of the teaching – and, indeed, non-teaching – staff, offering compensation for some of the unsatisfactory elements in working conditions and terms of employment.

Viewpoints and values

The entire educational process from the individual pupil's progress to the performance of the school as a whole is by-and-large a subjective matter. The opinions and evaluations of pupils themselves and all others involved in the work of the school reflect diverse interests, observations and knowledge, thus ranging from the casual and ignorant condemnation of it to the more objective and dispassionate. Managing in such a context must take account of all known viewpoints and values while steering the school to a position which commands the supportive judgement of the political majority.

On many issues, members of the teaching staff and governors are likely to take a similar view. If the school is relatively undisturbed by external pressures, a harmonious and happy working atmosphere is likely to develop. This is more likely to happen if the school is small and well led, but with good leadership it can also happen in large schools. However, the issues which arise in any school vary in number, complexity and severity. The school's exposure to external influences is great enough in most cases to generate a continual stream of issues. These all have to be faced and a constant process of internal adjustment to the school must be undertaken by its management.

In this case it is probable that different views about a variety of professional issues are to be found among the members of the teaching staff of a school. Sometimes, these views are very strongly held and with a conviction which makes it difficult to achieve a common policy and to carry out an agreed set of practices. This may lead to tension and frustration, which add extra strain to the task of teaching.

Different views may arise quite simply from a misunderstanding or from a lack of information. Provided goodwill exists, misunderstandings can be cleared up if appropriate steps are taken, and the lack of information can be rectified by making the necessary information available. Goodwill, however, does not always exist and it is not uncommon to find that different viewpoints cannot be reconciled easily. Staff may attribute the views of a particular colleague to eccentricity and be able to accommodate them with good humour, especially when a matter of principle is not at stake. When matters of principle *are* at stake it is not easy to shrug off the views of a colleague in such a tolerant way. Differences may persist and generate rancour, leading ultimately to low morale, disengagement and, finally, even schism.

Schools are not alone in experiencing the constant need to reconcile different viewpoints of principle and practice. It is a commonplace experience in organizations to find that other people do not always take the same view of an event or make the same appraisal of a situation as oneself. This happens even when the event or situation seems perfectly clear and unambiguous in nature. 'The realities which one person experiences seem inescapable to him though they clash with the realities which bind another person' (Greenfield 1977:92).

When events and situations are complex in nature and difficult to understand, most people are ready to accept differences of view – at least in the initial stage. People often ask one another, 'What do you make of it?' or 'Why do you take this view?' or 'Do you agree with this analysis?' Indeed, 'second opinions' are valued and sometimes raised to virtuous heights in some professions. In organizations, willingness to welcome and engage in the free exchange and appropriation of ideas and practices is the central concept of 'open systems thinking', which many people advocate as vital for the achievement of a happy, healthy and successful organization – particularly in education (Halpin 1966). An organization based on 'open systems thinking' recognizes the existence of different viewpoints and tries to use them as a capital asset for the benefit of the organization – rather than trying to ignore them or hoping they will go away in due course.

The differences of view which teachers exhibit may sometimes be attributed to sheer 'cussedness'. When viewpoints are genuine, and sincerely held, however, it is possible for members to see their own organization and the issues which arise in it in very different ways. They may cling to these different views and still remain devoted to the school, respectively determined to support it in every way they can. Such differences result from the fact that the cognitive abilities and psychological composition of each person are the products of varying congenital and environmental factors. Thus, distinctive viewpoints become characteristic of different individuals.

It is possible, but insensitive, for management to ignore the existence of these characteristic differences of view among organization members as a fundamental condition of 'corporate' or collective effort. To do so is not likely to lead to success. Managerial behaviour is more likely to be successful if two needs are borne in mind. In the first place, a managing teacher must be able to know, to recognize and to take account of the characteristic points of view of those with whom he or she works. Secondly, and of equal importance, a teacher engaged in managing beyond the classroom must surely know and take into account his or her *own* propensities or characteristic points of view.

Different views are based on different values. Insofar as differences become characteristic of the members of an organization they may be regarded as an asset or a hindrance

The rest of this chapter offers an identification, explanation and classification of the various habitual points of view which are found in practice and the premises upon which they are based. The resulting map of these viewpoints shows the range of fundamental positions which teachers take in schools. It shows that characteristically different positions which are taken produce characteristically different responses to the changing circumstances, challenges and reactions which organizational life produces.

The inclusive model devised for the purpose includes various material from other sources which has been adapted and supplemented. The first part of the model shows how individuals try to understand the organization of which they are members, particularly as a working whole. Individuals are influenced in their perceptions of complex organization by factors in life which are familiar and more immediate to them. Consequently, the human body, human family life and the manifest power and efficiency of machines of all kinds become objects of reference in a person's attempts to comprehend organization as a single entity.

The second part of the model draws on the imagery associated with the familiar experience of travel. It is concerned with how people view the positions which others take. The traveller has a changing relationship with the terrain. At various points on the path a different view of the same scene can be obtained. By analogy, organization members are at different points on the path of their experience in life in general and the organization in which they currently work in particular. Consequently, their views of the organization can be different from one another. This part of the model, therefore, shows how each person tends to view other individuals who are fellow members of the same organization. Significantly different personal viewpoints are identified and their practical outcomes classified.

The third and final part of the model sets out the main areas of personal values and preferences. It is concerned, therefore, with knowing oneself as an organization member and of being able to recognize one's own viewpoint and the fundamental premises upon which that viewpoint is based. The complete model is represented in tabular form at the end of the chapter (Table 1.1).

Understanding the whole school

Understanding anything implies conceptual grasp, which involves the aggregation of many parts into a whole or 'higher integration', and giving the latter some kind of meaning. An organization by definition is a synthesis of elements. An understanding of organization implies an appreciation of the whole and its constituent parts together with its purpose or function.

The human body.   It occasions no surprise that the human body should act as a catalyst in the search for an understanding of the organizational aspects of human life. The first factor that individuals notice is the unitary nature of the body. The second is that the wholeness of the body seems to be more than the sum of the parts. The malfunction or loss of a part is an impairment of the whole, the design of which assumes the indispensability of each part. Every part is different but every part counts. It is the function of each part to perform its characteristic task – no more and no less.

The projection of the body as an aid to achieving an understanding of organization has longstanding antecedents. For example, St Paul wrote to the church he had founded in Corinth: 'There are many different organs, but one body. The eye cannot say to the hand, "I do not need you"; nor the head to the feet, "I do not need you". Quite the contrary: those organs of the body which seem to be more frail than others are indispensable' (I Corinthians, Ch. 12).

In the modern age organic theories of organizations echo the principles implicit in such a view. Organization, consisting of many members, like a body, is a developing, adaptive phenomenon. It has increasing 'self-awareness' or 'consciousness' and may assume large powers of self-direction. But its members vary in their ability to make a contribution to the whole. Membership is, therefore, earned and based on merit, since the willingness to contribute varies as well as the ability.

Organizational health is a fluctuating condition and the ill-health of organizational parts sooner or later affects the whole. A 'sick' or malfunctioning member should not be removed, however, but retrained or given therapy in the form of retraining to enable him to resume making a normal and suitable contribution. Surgery in organization, as with the body, is only the last, desperate step.

If these are some of the characteristics of the 'organic' view of organization, it may be said that the perspective adopted is that of competency. In organizational terms, this is a matter of achieving a suitable deployment of differential ability among the organization members so that together a complex task can be undertaken.

> The human body offers a model for the understanding of organization which emphasizes the competency of its members deployed on the basis of differential ability

The human family.   The smallest organization has always been familiar to man in the form of the human family, particularly in its extended form. The salient features of the family are features which may be projected into larger groupings of people or organizations. In the family there is interdependence. Complementary factors are at work. The main feature, however, is the inequality of capacity – physical, intellectual and socio-emotional – of its members.

Parents do not 'choose' their children and offspring do not 'choose' their parents – an arbitrary factor is at work which is coupled with a dependency factor. The notion of authority exists to cope with these related factors. Authority provides support for inadequate parents and helps curb the excesses of rebellious children. The hardness of authority, however, is softened by the simultaneous recognition of the family as a forum of trust, the expression of warmth and the toleration of idiosyncrasies.

The school as an organization is sometimes viewed as a very large family. Its family aspects may be energetically promoted and tenaciously defended. In such cases there would be a strong concern by status-conscious individuals to preserve a paternalistic or maternalistic regime. This in essence provides protection, patronage and reward in return for recognition of authority on the grounds of convention, titles and ranks, but not necessarily merit. The assumption of offices and powers in the organization is derivative in origin. Individuals are expected to be sensitive to their status or positions, and their concomitant authority.

In the school viewed as a family, tasks emanate progressively to larger numbers of people as a result of the decisions of progressively fewer people and, possibly, ultimately one person – the patron or 'father' of the organization – the head of school. The essential characteristic in this case is that of delegation. In the family each member may have particular responsibilities. Typically, as a family grows so the older children are expected to assume greater responsibilities. Delegation assumes a larger vision, greater wisdom and more knowledge on the part of the one person or the few upon whom the many depend for sustenance and inspiration. In operational terms, the organizational emphasis provided by the family as a model is the deployment of formal authority among organization members, by which each is enabled to carry out his or her part of the total work of the organization.

> The human family offers a model for the understanding of organization which emphasizes the delegation of responsibilities to its members deployed according to the formal authority they have been given

The world of nature.   Beyond the body and family is the natural environment of one's existence. This, too, provides powerful formative influences. One's perception of the world of nature may lead to a variety of interpretations but the general existence of flora and fauna is an inescapable element of the context of human life and a potential determinant of attitudes, not least by the idea of conservation.

The ebb and flow or cyclical character of the seasons is an impressive feature. This is the effect of external factors upon plants and animals, shaping the stimuli to which they must respond and providing the basic terms of survival. But within and between the species there is a pattern of existence in terms of their incidence or distribution relative to opportunity.

Many may perceive this as a subtle balance between existing species – the ecological view. This is to emphasize the aspect of overall good order, the total pattern and synthesis which proves to be viable. On the other hand, many perceive the synthesis in terms of the experience of the individual animal or plant involved. This is to emphasize the struggle which the elemental parts of the natural world are inescapably involved in to establish themselves and survive.

In organizations both of these perceptions are expressed in the concept of dominance. The manifestations of attitudes moulded by this perception would be a deployment of natural power. The dominant ones determine what happens. One might go as far as Hobbes in the *Leviathan* and depict social life without any governmental constraints as 'nasty, brutish and short'. Without the dominant ones, therefore, modern organizations might well become vehicles of unbridled savagery where 'every man's hand is against every man'. When a senior teacher in a London comprehensive school was informed of a television programme which related the hazardous early life of newly born turtles he commented 'that is how it is for all of us', as if the dominance order was insufficiently established and defined to prevent continual and arbitrary harassment from all quarters.

On the other hand, the organization might be regarded as an instrument for mitigating the excesses, whilst dealing with the fact, of the struggle for dominance. Organizational life is perforce constantly stimulating. The necessary adjustments of individuals and sub-groups are variously successful. The weaker give way to the stronger and a dominance pattern – however disguised – emerges. This is an irresistible process and precipitates a constant potential for instability – as evident among teachers in their work in schools as anywhere else.

> The world of nature offers a model for the understanding of organization which emphasizes the dominance of members deployed according to their natural powers

The machine.   Mechanical devices of all kinds have become commonplace as extensions of the human body's powers for both work and leisure.

They generate as much interest as the body itself. The very principles which can so evidently facilitate the invention and use of the machine may be projected for use into other spheres of concern, notably human organization. The characteristics of the machine are demonstrable and normally irrefutable. There can be objectivity, therefore, and agreement, between people over a machine's construction and function. Furthermore, whilst the malfunctioning of one of its parts may reduce the efficiency of the machine sooner or later, each part is more readily and ethically detachable and replaceable than the human body. The authenticity of the function of the machine as a whole and any of its constituent parts can be viewed with unemotional detachment.

In organizations, the attitudes which rely on the efficacy of the machine pay due tribute to the scientific outlook of the modern age. They look to the concept of rationality in organization. Identifiable parts have specific functions and must discharge them or be discarded. Interchangeable parts or flexibility of functions is an important demand. There is a strong emphasis on efficiency – the matching of inputs or resources with output or product. It betrays a skill-conscious or effectiveness-in-action attitude. Skill takes precedence over personality and, therefore, rationality over patronage. Operationally this attitude would result in a deployment of technical tasks, favoured by those in teaching who seek to secure an extensive measure of control over the organization and anathema to those who fear or deplore such attempts at precision.

> The machine offers a model for the understanding of organization
> which emphasizes rationality among members deployed according to
> the technical functions to be discharged

Understanding the viewpoints of others

Organizations loom large in the landscape of human life and have an important bearing on the individual's search for meaning (Frankl 1967). As life, like a journey, proceeds, an accumulation of experiences – some significant, some insignificant – contribute towards the development of an individual's personal view of it. Each new experience in turn acts as an opportunity for either adaptive or maladaptive behaviour. This process may become stressful and it is the concern of many to seek a suitable standpoint which will provide a sense of stability and sanity. An ability to recognize the characteristic viewpoints of others is essential if a senior teacher wishes to work successfully at a managerial level. Some of these are typified as follows. They have been characterized by Furlong (1973) as the *Comic View*, the *Romantic View*, the *Ironic View* and the *Tragic View*.

Comic view.   Those who are persuaded of the efficacy of selected 'gospels' are said to have a comic view of life. The view is comical because it belongs to the pretentious posturings of those who deify a particular cognitive system or philosophical approach as the definitive answer to man's search for meaning and an understanding of the cosmos. Thus the claims of politics, science, technology, behavioural psychology, medicine and similar fields of study when taken in isolation amount to so many entertaining but essentially 'trivial' antics. They are especially regarded as such when they attempt to postulate 'progress' and take a highly abstracted, linear and 'short-cut' view of the complexity of life. There is a constant need to take a whole view and to allow for the basic inability of our finite minds to be able to comprehend the infinite. The comic view *is* comic because there would appear to be an implicit pride and unjustified assurance where none is warranted.

In schools the comic visionary is a person given to the habit of offering mechanistic solutions to all kinds of problems. There is a fondness for precision, prescription and prediction on the basis of a simple conceptualization of cause and effect. There is a love of tidiness and a resistance to muddle. There is a fatal confusion between the intuitive grasp of a complex situation, as may be communicated to others in relatively uncomplicated terms, and the actual implementation of measures which need to be taken as a corrective. The future, it is thought, may be programmed fully and accomplished without delay. No account is taken of the arbitrary and sometimes perverse nature of people in organizations. The uncertainties of school life in particular defy the direct solutions of the comic visionary.

> The comic view is that which offers unidimensional explanations of organizational problems

Romantic view.   In contrast, the romantic view is essentially retrospective rather than prospective. In the experience of those who take a romantic view there exists a perceived reality or condition which exerts a magnetic hold over their emotions. It is inevitably an abstraction, constructed in the image of a unique pattern of personal needs. It represents a perpetual rejection of the *status quo* and an assertion of superiority of view in that the preferred interpretation of the past is in some way specially possessed and undertsood by the romantic. His attitude of hostility or alienation to the present implies a deprivation which is counterbalanced by the privilege derived from his position of interpreter of a past golden age that can be revived as a solution to the problems of the present.

The romantic visionary in organizations is doctrinaire in the sense that modifications take their cue not from what the situation demands but from what his blue-print demands. It inevitably implies a maladaptive attitude, with a resistance to change, since the criteria chosen for taking and judging action are rooted at worst in prejudice and possibly the recovery of vested interest, previous status and influence. At best they signal the hope of recovery of preferred values which have declined in general esteem.

> The romantic view is that which measures present organizational problems against a preferred interpretation of the past

Ironic view. The essential element in the make-up of those who take the ironic view is that of detachment, with a resistance to commitment. Psychic energy is derived from not taking oneself or others too seriously. Of course there is the possibility that detachment might mean unconcern or even complacency. Rather than the result of stoical self-discipline, it might appear in practice as a form of self-indulgence akin to aristocratic superiority, facilitated by financial and social security. Detachment could be regarded as the product variously of age – and so of fatigue, of maturity – and so of wisdom, or it could be regarded as being of therapeutic self-analysis – and so of survival strategy.

In organizations, the divide between those who seek change for whatever reasons and those who oppose change for whatever reasons often seems unbridgeable. Detachment then appears to parade as conservatism which is interpreted as complacency or indifference. It is the perennial struggle between the imagined 'haves and have-nots' in organizations – whether cast in terms of incomes, participation or advancement.

Teaching as a whole is regarded by some other sectors of employment as being in the grip of those with an ironic view, or detachment, about the shape and condition of life outside the school. A union leader in the United States once said of teachers that one of the prime troubles, if not the chief curse of the teaching profession was that teachers too often took a detached view of the problems that assail society. '. . . your craft is somewhat above this world of ours; it implies a remoteness from the daily battle of the streets, the neighbourhood and the cities. . . .' (Quoted by Stinnett 1968:353).

The over-exposure to stimulation and the sanity of detachment are possibilities to which everyone in organizations is subject. The reply to jibes that the ironic view is characteristic of the successful and those who wish to preserve the *status quo* can only be in terms of the obvious. At any given point of time there are certain features of an organization which any one individual *can* change – but a vast number which he or she *cannot* change. Nowhere is this more true than of teachers in the school, whatever the positions they hold.

> The ironic view is that which urges detachment in coping with organizational problems

Tragic view. The essential feature in the tragic view is the recognition that the inescapable human predicament consists of dashed hopes, disappointed faith and unsatisfied yearnings. Yet to make no effort at all is self-destructive – the individual may have to learn to accept an unhappy suspension between mutually disagreeable positions. In making such an effort, however, the individual is exposed to the dangers, terrors and mysteries of the risk in addition to the basic dilemmas of paradox and ambiguity. Those who make the effort are the heroic ones, the tragic figures striving against great odds.

In organizations, the tragic hero is often the awkward individual who seems to delight in attracting hostility and to relish choosing arguments and positions which are bound to generate animosity towards him. It is a lonely stance. If taken by an obscure member of the organization it attracts the limelight to the individual and he can be made into a scapegoat. If taken by the powerful in an organization it rapidly crystallizes opinion. People resent the distant figure at the top and dislike being reminded dramatically of the dilemmas in their own lives.

The individual who takes the tragic view is in constant danger of generating impossible odds to derive a deep satisfaction from non-attainment and self-justification, as if resistant to solutions. Members of organizations need to recognize the virtues of accepting the limitations of reality but of responding courageously to the complexities of existence in organizations at the same time, without turning it into a crusade.

> The tragic view is that which points out the inevitability of failure in dealing with organizational problems

Understanding one's own viewpoint

One of the abiding subjects of interest in education is the nature of truth. At some time or other teachers are obliged to consider the question of what is true knowledge and to be concerned that pupils should think about the nature of truth and to value truth. What is truth? The historical question of Pontius Pilate cannot be given an answer with which all would agree.

At the back of a person's views about anything in life there are always some fundamental assumptions. These are clearly of critical importance in any attempt to account for differences of views in the school and in the efforts made to manage it as an organization constructively and effectively. The final part of this chapter is reserved for the identification and description of five critical value systems which are found among teachers. These are called *Idealism, Realism, Rationalism, Experimentalism* and *Existentialism*. They are presented in summary form. (Morris 1961; Butler 1966; Bayles 1966; Lawson 1957; Morris 1966; Laing 1967; Hughes 1976; Greenfield 1977).

Idealism.   If a person is prone to view objects perceived by the senses as imperfect manifestations of what they *might* be, then that person may be said to be an idealist. The 'might be' here refers to the perfect form of the object which in fact exists not in terms of tangible reality but may do so as an *idea* or *ideal* in the mind of the observer.

All objects, whether inanimate or animate, non-human or human, are considered in relation to the perfected form which can be apprehended and understood by mind alone. Behind all persons, therefore, there is the *idea* of personhood which acts as a reference and touchstone for all thoughts about persons. It actively governs the ways in which an idealist regards a particular person and interacts with him.

For example, a teacher with a grasp of the world of *ideas* would be able to penetrate the 'sensory screen' which surrounds a child and 'see' the ideal which that child might become. To close the gap between the ideal and the actual is impossible by definition, but the possibility of reducing the distance serves as a mainspring for action and judgement.

As far as organizations are concerned, the idealist's position would be that relatively few members of an organization are able to 'see' what an organization as an entity might become. Such people have a drive towards perfection. The alleged possession of the view of the *ideal*, however, does not necessarily imply that the observer has a comprehensive grasp of the existing condition of a particular organization at any point of time. Still less does it imply the capability to correct the composition and course of an organization in accord with that ideal. Above all, however, stands the vexed issue as to whether a vision of the ideal implies any special prescriptive *right* to assume powers to attempt corrective courses of action beyond those attaching to other members of the organization in question.

> Idealism is the tendency to emphasize organization as what it *should* be

Realism. A person persuaded of the importance of natural law does so in the belief in the demonstrable fact that man is himself only part of the cosmos. His powers are strictly finite in a realm of powers which he did not originate and cannot change. The laws which operate in the universe govern all phenomena including the human being and the social predicament. The intelligent way to proceed – and this strategy itself can be seen as a natural law – is to seek to discover the underlying and pervasive laws at work in any prescribed material or human event or series of events.

Man can discover the laws and work with them for his own accommodation. He can work against them only at his peril. Events are 'out there' to be observed. They are neither good nor bad apart from whether or not they are the result of the operations of natural law.

The realist teacher is one inclined to accept what he sees as 'the facts of life' such as the ineradicable differences of ability, interest, potential power and prosperity of individuals. In his organization, the realist will accept what *is* the case rather than emphasize what *might* be the case as the idealist does. He proceeds by way of finding out what is working in practice on the basis of careful observations of the relevant natural laws which permit it to do so. Predictability is the hallmark of realism. There is a drive towards order.

The claim of individuals to be able to discover the natural laws and communicate their findings to others in respect of organizations is as awesome as the claim of idealists to have had a vision of the ideal. Incontestable capability would be omniscience indeed. The natural laws may in fact in *themselves* be absolute, but the frailty and imperfection of human perception, knowing and communicating are 'natural' constraints on any over-weening pretentions of the realist's analysis and correction of organizational ills.

> Realism is the tendency to emphasize organization as that which actually exists

Rationalism.   Rationalism takes its stand on the claim that the cosmos is a logical construction. The human mind as part of the cosmos is logical in nature and functions as a special means for comprehending the universe. It does so characteristically by intuition – that is, by the immediate and direct act of understanding.

The facts or truth of a situation are, therefore, self-evident. Once an individual understands by intuition, he or she must then undertake the task of analysis or deductive reasoning, utilizing the logic which is inherent in any question or problem under review as a means for doing so.

In his organizational commitments the rational person looks for the overview or grasp of the whole, supported by a rigorous discipline of analysis for the purpose of elaboration and communication, with rationality in all things. In their views on the curriculum, rationalist teachers are more likely to support well-structured subjects like mathematics than subjects which permit arbitrary structure.

In organizations, the pre-eminence given to logic in both the intellectual and practical spheres predisposes the rationalist to a drive towards making hierarchies. Hierarchy has singularly important implications for the construction and running of organizations. It is self-evident that if the finite powers of man are attempting to cope with the infinite variety of reality, then a rational distribution of effort is needed. Given the purpose, then each person concerned must be assigned a place and responsibility in the organization. One person is logically related to another and retained in position either by self-discipline or externally applied means.

The implicit assumptions of firmness of purpose and stability of organizational arrangements in the rationalist's attitude easily attract charges of vested interest. More seriously, however, in times of rapid change they appear to many to be wilfully maladaptive.

> Rationalism is the tendency to emphasize organizations as a matter of logic

Experimentalism. This 'colossus of our age' is also called pragmatism or instrumentalism. Reality to the experimentalist is always in flux. Experience is the only worthwhile measure of reality. This consists of conscious interaction between the human being and other people or objects – all of which are part and parcel of the 'real' world. The experimentalist has a drive towards participation.

Since such experience must inevitably vary from person to person, truth about the cosmos or any part of it must always be temporary, tentative and subject always to 'another view' – itself based upon a different experience. Knowledge is freely made and unmade. It is not fixed and final. Unlike the realist who may feel that consensus is possible in the face of objective 'facts' – that is, the discovery of the natural law and how it operates – the experimentalist stresses the subjective nature of knowledge. It is personal in the sense that it results from individual experience and is the best available knowledge to work with 'until something better comes along'.

The important caveat is that the position taken by an experimentalist is not a pretentious one like that taken by an idealist or a realist. An individual says in effect: 'This is how I find things. I am waiting for the fresh experience of others or myself that will persuade me to change my view.' The experimentalist's position is essentially open to change and, therefore, implies the public nature of knowledge and a free dissemination of views. Knowledge is inevitably a synthesis of views. Though an individual may find a particular synthesis to be disagreeable, it is nonetheless acknowledged as the best knowledge available for the time being.

In organizations an experimentalist proceeds by way of acting on what is known at the present and by studying the consequences of any actions taken. This observation leads to a 'reconstruction of experience'. The individual then uses these consequences as new raw material for the contemplation of further action and a basis for postulating how to implement decisions taken. In the jargon of scientific method, the experimentalist first takes a given situation as a 'problem' because it contains unsatisfactory elements. He then makes an inventory of solutions, including the possible and the improbable and conjectures the consequences of each in turn. In testing the impact made by each by an 'experiment' or 'pilot scheme' he eliminates all but the best which then becomes fully implemented and maintained. Because it works it is 'right' and certainly acceptable to the experimentalist. It is in turn, however, not a final solution but only an interim accommodation.

> Experimentalism is the tendency to emphasize organization as a matter of what works

Existentialism.   The cardinal factor for the existentialist is the absolute power of choice. Whatever data are assembled and by whatever means and on whatever subject, the fact remains that each individual for whatever reasons possess the inalienable power of choice to accept or reject them. Individual choice is the ultimate arbiter. No person nor set of circumstances intrinsically carries an inescapable and superordinate power to compel conviction and obedience. The drive of the existentialist is towards diversification.

Being conscious of the fact that he or she *is* conscious, the existentialist assumes that he or she is squarely confronted with an indivisible obligation of personal responsibility. He or she cannot 'blame' someone else for his or her predicament. Being responsible for one's actions is of the essence. A prior investigation of the possible consequences of an action before it is taken is, therefore, an implied requirement in existentialist thinking.

In organizations existentialists recognize no authority and no duty other than those they choose to recognize. There is no consideration that such recognitions ought to be made. In a school, for example, the adoption of educational and resource objectives and professional performance criteria carries no automatic power to compel agreement and support. This is particularly so when the existentialist teacher has played no part in deciding what they should be. Even if such a teacher had taken part in deciding what they should be, however, the existentialist in that teacher could still make it possible subsequently to choose to repudiate the arrangements made. There is no 'moral' duty to stand by them – only a consideration of the consequence of the particular choice made. However strongly supported a measure may be, the awesome face of collective decision does not pre-empt personal power of choice in the matter.

> Existentialism is the tendency to emphasize organization as what
> members choose to accept

Teachers may think about their schools as organizations in very different ways. When issues arise in schools, they generate different viewpoints, which are based upon different values of fundamental importance and priority to the individuals concerned. These can account for very different assessments of given circumstances and will lead to different preferences as solutions to the same problem. Those who occupy positions of managerial importance are included in this – they too have particular and characteristic views of reality. Organization must inevitably accommodate these differences in one way or another. Differences of view and different

Table 1.1 Inclusive model of viewpoints and values

| *Understanding the whole school* | | |
Viewpoint	*Value*	*Organizational outcome*
Human body	Competency	Deployment of differential ability
Human family	Delegation	Deployment of formal authority
World of nature	Dominance	Deployment of natural power
Machine	Rationality	Deployment of technical tasks
Understanding the viewpoints of others		
Viewpoint	*Value*	*Organizational outcome*
Comic view	Definitive explanations	Resistance to muddle
Romantic view	Recovery of former state	Resistance to change
Ironic view	Detachment	Resistance to commitment
Tragic view	Inevitable paradox	Resistance to solutions
Understanding one's own viewpoint		
Viewpoint	*Value*	*Organizational outcome*
Idealism	Mental process	Drive towards perfection
Realism	Natural law	Drive towards order
Rationalism	Intuition	Drive towards hierarchy
Experimentalism	Experience	Drive towards participation
Existentialism	Choice	Drive towards diversification

values may be regarded as a hindrance or as an asset in the management of organization.

A number of ways of trying to understand what organizations are like as entities, the view one may take of the viewpoints of others, and the values which affect one's own views, have been identified and described. These are embodied in an inclusive model, summarized as Table 1.1, p. 31.

2 The work of schools

An organization exists when two or more people deliberately share a common purpose. Without organization, complex human purposes cannot be fulfilled. This is obviously true in the case of field sports or in producing a domestic refrigerator or in operating a commercial aircraft. Similarly, in a school where there is a need to provide competent teaching in a wide range of areas for a large number of pupils, the cooperative activity of many people is required. The task is not an easy one and has often been underestimated, as illustrated in the following unsolicited and verbatim commentary. This was made by a person who had completed a higher degree and worked in educational administration for a local authority before entering teaching.

> When I actually spent time in two schools, it was brought home very forcefully to me that teaching at this level is not so simple and easy as those who lecture on degree level physics and business studies courses had assumed that it was. To ensure that children have mastered basic skills like reading, writing and arithmetic, are developing their physical and emotional skills and are becoming socialised into the community is an exceedingly complicated and demanding task.

The need for common ground

The important condition of organization lies in the existence of common purpose. This implies at least a degree of recognition of common purpose by each person involved. Insofar as that recognition is explicit and strong, the potential for the survival and prosperity of the organization is good. When such recognition is half-hearted or weak, the organization's potential for survival and prosperity is correspondingly poor.

In the case of schools the need is to balance the school's *consensual* function and its *differentiating* function. The consensual function is concerned with those activities, procedures and judgements which are involved in the transmission of values and their derived norms, making for shared experience and outlook, which have a potentially cohesive social effect. On returning from a visit to a school, a postgraduate student-teacher wrote the following comment (quoted verbatim): 'I was very struck by the community feeling within the school, and realise how closely this is related to the school's aim that children will have respect for one another, and become caring members of the community (in school, and the wider outside community).' The differentiating function is concerned with those activities, procedures and judgements which are involved in the pupil's acquisition of specific skills and knowledge which have a potentially divisive effect (Bernstein, Elvin and Peters 1966).

Consequently, the object of concern in the school is to find sufficient common ground so that the education of the pupils may be effectively carried out. It must be remembered, however, that schools are not the sole suppliers of learning. In the process of education the school is no more than a contributor, even though it is a very important one. The family itself is the child's first 'school' though learning in it may be fragmentary and unsystematic – deficiencies which the teacher seeks to correct in providing a purposeful, routinized and rounded learning programme. Other institutions have an interest and an influence too. Schools then do not hold a monopoly of interest and decision in the matter of the pupil's life chances. The common ground which must be found to provide the school with the unity it needs as an organization, therefore, cannot be defined by the teaching staff alone. The pupils, in undertaking their study, are not passive in the process of education; and parents as well as employers have an interest in what takes place since they must accommodate it. Furthermore, whilst the financial cost of schooling in the public sector continues to be borne by taxpayers from national and local taxation, government at national and local levels is involved in a fundamental way. The national government frames legislation for schools and provides over half the finance. Local government supplies the rest of the finance and generally controls the schools in its area by means of policy directives, rules, regulations and advice. The right of schools to opt out of local government control established in the Education Reform Act of 1988 and subsequently extended to include even small primary schools potentially reduces or eliminates the ties between the school and local government. By the same token it strengthens the ties between the school and national government which supplies all its finances, except that which is raised by the school's own private initiative.

There are four parties to the educational contract, therefore – the pupil as 'doer', the parent and employer as 'user', the teacher as 'provider' and government as 'facilitator'. Each party has a different interest and perspective, all of which must be reconciled if the organization is to act as a unity to achieve a common and recognized or accepted set of purposes.

> The four parties to the educational contract are
> - the pupil as 'doer'
> - the parent and employer as 'user'
> - the teacher as 'provider'
> - the government as 'facilitator'

Among any group of pupils, their parents or potential employers and the teachers associated with a particular school, there is inevitably a wide range of different personal purposes to be served. The range can be so wide and contain so many mutually exclusive elements that some observers have been led to conclude that schools should be conceived as organized anarchies. From the point of view of those who manage the school the essential need is for processes by which enough common ground can be identified and thereafter maintained and modified. The energies of everyone in the organization need to be marshalled and effectively focused on achieving the educational outcomes that represent the task of the organization. In this sense the school is a unitary organization.

The energies of the teaching staff form the critical factor in the school as an organization; 'in the last resort only teachers can make any educational system work well' (Department of Education and Science 1965: para. 41). In theory they should be unified and directed unambiguously towards the education of the pupil. In practice energy is lost to this purpose in two ways. In the first place, some of it is diverted from the primary task to cope with internal complexities and breakdowns of organization. These include many things from form-filling to attending meetings, political adjudication and healing rifts between staff members. Taken together, they represent *organization maintenance costs*. An illustration of organization maintenance costs – perceived as being too high – is contained in the following copy of a letter by a teacher to a national newspaper. Incidentally, it also illustrates the change which has taken place in the assumptions of teachers to be able to give expression to their opinion on educational matters in public – presumably with impunity. Teachers have been subject to disciplinary action if they engaged in such public dialogue, particularly if the matter of discussion concerned the local education authority's policy or the teacher's own school.

> . . . those who teach least get paid most.
>
> In large comprehensive schools such as the one where I teach the senior staff are given a much lighter 'teaching-load' because they have numerous administrative duties to perform. Almost all of these such as arranging examination timetables, parents' evenings, substitutions for absent staff, allocation of rooms, collating information on a vast range of topics, and, most time-consuming of all, the drawing-up of the school timetable, could

be done as well, if not better, by someone employed in a purely administrative capacity.

One such person, who would need to be nothing more than an efficient administrator, could relieve senior teachers of all their non-teaching tasks, except those concerning curriculum policy, discipline and pupils' welfare . . .

(The *Daily Telegraph* 1979)

Many innovations and modifications in recent years have led to an increase in organization maintenance costs. Notably, the struggle over the introduction of pupil testing in the National Curriculum was in part due to fears about the inordinate increase of such costs. Any system requiring documentation means time added to teaching contact time. This is true for homework, forecasts, teaching preparations, costings and pupil records or profiling as well as pupil testing and even staff appraisal. They all put pressure on the teacher's working week and may encroach unreasonably on the teacher's private life. Such organization maintenance costs may be seen as arising from shifts in the values and expectations of the wider community and therefore unavoidable. From a strictly managerial point of view they need to be viewed in product terms. As well as being *cost-efficient* or cheap in themselves relative to their value in use, they need to be *cost-effective* or able to add an increment of benefit or improvement to the product which means raising the educational standards of the pupil.

In the second place, the energies of the teaching staff can be diverted from their primary purpose to cope with the complaints and criticisms from outside sources, as well as events which affect the school directly but over which they have no control. These include such matters as bad publicity, community policies, strike action, legal procedures and vandalism. Taken together, they represent *organization defence costs*. Distractions for the school may arise from many sources – high-level national disputes, local initiative to stir up support for particular policies and, at institutional level, the actions of those who subject the school to too many extraneous and contradictory influences. These sources of distraction create organization defence costs.

There are increasing expectations of personal discretion and freedom of expression among both teachers and pupils or their parents. Social values and attitudes affect the terms on which organizational unity are based. They must be accommodated internally and used to achieve the educational task of the school. Such changes must not be allowed to cause organization maintenance costs to run rampant. Similarly, schools have seldom been exposed to greater scrutiny with regard to both economic costs of educational programmes and the content of those programmes. Official and unofficial bodies both formally and informally seek to influence schools. Again, such changes must be accommodated without distracting the energies of the teaching staff by raising organization defence costs.

Those who manage the school as an organization always have a major responsibility. It is to ensure that all possible energy is devoted to the organization's primary task. This outcome can be achieved by reducing the energy loss incurred by organization maintenance and defence to the lowest levels possible. This responsibility as a factor in organizational effectiveness is illustrated in Fig. 2.1, which visually combines and interrelates the main ideas contained in this chapter.

Interpreting the task through objectives

The task of the organization may be understood in terms of the socially recognized reason for the organization's existence. The task is *given* to the organization rather than created by it, and is sanctioned in the legal, economic and fiscal policies of the community. The task given to the school is usually implied or conveyed in vague or ambiguous terms, relying heavily on convention and tacit understandings. The professional skill of the school lies in its ability to articulate this task, to make it explicit and to make it work. This involves the interpretation of the hopes and aspirations of the community so that constructive action can be taken to fulfil them.

The work of the school, therefore, can only proceed effectively when the task which the community assigns to it has been interpreted sufficiently accurately and with sufficient precision. The school needs to embody its interpretation in a form which everyone understands and which provides a general guide for concrete action. The form taken is a set of *interpretative task statements*, often called aims.

Such interpretative task statements need to be formulated and given order of priority. A sample set of interpretative task statements in random order is contained in Table 2.1.

The interpretative task statements in Table 2.1 are confined to the outcomes which the school will be able to effect in the pupil. The use of a finite list such as this has the singular advantage of providing a common measure for comparing the broad priorities of the various parties to the educational contract – the pupils, the parents and employers, the teachers and the government. Significant differences and similarities of interest among these different parties to the educational contract have been shown to exist in actual schools when they have been asked to express their priorities in terms of the eighteen items.

The need for a school to interpret the task assigned to it by the community and to formulate its interpretation in a set of clear statements which may be conveyed to everyone concerned and understood by them, is of self-evident importance. All members of the organization should be

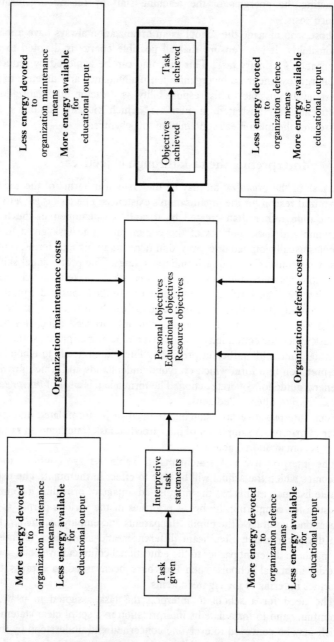

Figure 2.1 Objectives and effective organization

Table 2.1 Sample set of interpretative task statements

Learn how to be a good citizen
Learn how to respect and get along with people who think, dress and act
    differently
Learn about and try to understand the changes that take place in the world
Develop skills in reading, writing, speaking and listening
Understand and practise democratic ideas and ideals
Learn how to examine and use information
Understand and practise the skills of family living
Learn to respect and get along with people with whom we work and live
Develop skills to enter a specific field of work
Learn how to be a good manager of money, property and resources
Develop a desire for learning, now and in the future
Learn how to use leisure time
Practise and understand the ideas of health and safety
Appreciate culture and beauty in the world
Gain information needed to make job selections
Develop pride in work and a feeling of self-worth
Develop good character and self-respect
Gain a general education

Source: Phi Delta Kappa, Bloomington, Indiana

aware of these interpretations and be party to any changes which subsequently occur. They provide the ground for cooperative action and the intelligent conduct of individuals in the school. The process of underlining their importance begins for teachers during initial training, as the following extracts from reports on their teaching practice by two postgraduate student-teachers make plain. 'I had not really considered before how the aims and philosophy of the school must be clearly thought out and understood before that school can begin to function as a learning environment for children.' 'I had not really thought much about the importance of the overall aims and philosophy of a school.'

If the community conveys its wishes to the school in general and inexplicit terms, the school retains a corresponding measure of freedom of interpretation and action. This freedom at school level varies considerably from country to country. It is always open to the community to decide to be more explicit in its definition of the task.

Table 2.2 shows the interpretative task statement or aims current in a particular school, followed by the school's own initial interpretation by way of those organization and curriculum measures which need to be chosen to realize the stated aims. Departments or other sub-groups of teaching and non-teaching staff in turn provide detailed descriptions of the specific actions they will take to contribute to the realization of the school's aims, or what is expected of the school.

Table 2.2 An example of a school's published aims or interpretative task statement and initial description of how it will realize them

AIMS

The School aims to create, within a Christian framework, a caring and purposeful working environment which involves pupils fully in the learning experience and helps them to derive enjoyment from it. Importance is attached to development in all aspects of achievement to enable pupils to benefit fully from the opportunities of adult life and to face its challenges. They are encouraged to exercise self-discipline, initiative and consideration for others both in school and in the community. The school actively supports the policy of equal opportunities for all.

Organization and curriculum

1. Pupils are allocated, on admission, to one or four guilds, each in the charge of a senior member of staff who is responsible for the welfare and development of individual boys and girls throughout their school lives.
2. Each of the three deputies has a pastoral role; taking responsibility for either the lower school (years 1–3), the upper school (years 4–5) or the sixth form.
3. Pupils are placed in mixed-ability tutor groups within their year, each of which is affiliated to one of the four guilds to ensure a close-knit pastoral structure.
4. In the first and second year all subjects are taught to mixed-ability classes, but some setting is introduced from the third year onwards.
5. In years four and five examination courses are chosen by pupils and their parents, with advice and guidance from subject teachers and Guild Wardens. The basic core curriculum at this stage includes sessions on various aspects of careers education and strong links exist with the Careers Service; sex education forms part of an integrated health programme throughout the school, and emphasizes the importance of personal morality and the value of family life.
6. Support teaching and withdrawal groups operate to provide additional help for children with special educational needs.
7. Programmes are also arranged to extend and develop particular aptitudes shown by pupils.
8. As girls form only 25 per cent of pupil numbers considerable efforts are made to provide an environment in which girls have the confidence and opportunity to develop their strengths. Careful grouping arrangements, the recognition and display of girls' achievements and the monitoring of lesson materials are some of the methods used.
9. All pupils are expected to do homework regularly.
10. Religious education in the school is in accordance with the principles and practice of the Church of England. The schoool has its own School/ Community Liaison Officer who makes personal contact with the pupils' homes and close links are established with the London Borough of Tower Hamlets support services.
11. Discipline is maintained by supervision, by a consistent system of referral, by regular contact with parents and by the imposition of certain sanctions, if necessary.
12. Importance is attached to encouragement and to affording opportunities for pupils to exercise responsibility and initiative.

Source: Sir John Cass's Foundation and Red Coat Church of England Secondary School, London

Contemporary trends

In the closing years of the twentieth century the considerations which govern people's expectations of schools have become redefined and new elements have been included. Notably there is the belief that young people should be active rather than passive. Many people look to the oncoming generations, not only for a wider understanding of the society and its problems into which they are born but also in order to have a hand in shaping and preserving it.

At the beginning of the twentieth century Herbert Spencer left on record the argument that children and young people should be prepared by educational institutions to raise their own families and make and manage their own homes, to become adults and exercise the rights and obligations of citizenship, to play a full part in contributing to the common good in employment, and to occupy leisure time constructively and beneficially. A hundred years later the qualitative aspects of social life, environmental issues and strategies for survival concerning access to scarce resources are uppermost in the minds of many thoughtful people.

The preservation and improvement of the democratic form of society and government, already forged with such great effort are probably of foremost importance. This involves respecting and working for an elected parliament, politically neutral armed services, a professional civil service, an independent judiciary, a free press, a conservative education system, an industrial free market and non-discrimination in the case of sex, race, religion, and class.

Of all the concerns with which children and young people can be confronted perhaps none is be more important than that of needing to care for the global habitat of mankind. The first industrial revolution was the epoch in which the human race mastered the process of extracting goods from nature and turning them into useful commodities. This was the achievement of manufacture. The second industrial revolution was the epoch in which the human race mastered the processes of enabling ever increasing populations widely to share in the possession and use of those commodities through the growth of service mechanisms and industries. This was the achievement of distribution.

Neither epoch is historically clearly placed since the process involved is psychological as well as practical. They have overlapped and still are imperfectly achieved. But already in motion and added to them is the third industrial revolution in which the human race learns to master the processes of re-using discarded commodities after both productive and private use and ensuring that natural resources continue to yield some benefits. This is the achievement of reclamation. It requires scientific and artistic attitudes and skills equal to those which made the first two epochs possible together with sufficient investment, law and regulation to ensure that what is taken from nature is made to re-enter the manufacturing processes all over again for one purpose or another or is returned to nature in a harmless state.

Dominating much responsible thinking is the thought that development needs to be related to conservation. Wilderness can be a natural phenomenon with its own ecological basis but can also be created by people in the pursuit of development in a form which proves to be an ecological disaster – at least in the short term – if not accompanied by conservation policies. Such policies are vital when land has been used for the extraction of natural materials or ceases to be used for industrial purposes such as railways or manufacture, or when used for the dumping of waste. Building can be reclaimed and repaired. Many used materials can be recycled or given alternative uses. Renewable materials like timber need to be used at a rate which can be met by replacement. Energy can be saved by well-documented means and linked to the need to reduce pollution levels.

It may be the case that a set of general aims is developing which appeals to more and more countries in the contemporary world as they strive to make their education systems more adaptive to nations and international imperatives. They can be summarized as follows.

1. Promoting the country's economy – creating its wealth on a competitive footing.
2. Cultivating democratic and multi-racial society – fulfilling the obligations and using the rights of citizenship.
3. Training for domestic and family management – exercising the skills of building a home, a marriage, relationships and being a parent.
4. Establishing the knowledge and skills for health, safety and security – pursuing advisable habits and avoiding harmful practices and crime.
5. Developing intellectual and practical leisure pursuits – adding a range of interests to that of employment.
6. Protecting the environment – reducing pollution and preserving plants, animals and materials.

The work of the school is to raise the educational standards of whole populations by an appreciable percentage. This means producing a higher average level of knowledge and skills for personal, social and industrial use, more responsible conduct, and greater ability to adapt to changing conditions. In this task the school must find grounds for optimism and resist environmental pessimism, as is illustrated in the following passage.

The view of the future for most people is an exceptionally short-sighted one. . . . Successful planning is based on the premise that man will continue in the future to make the same mistakes that he made in the past. While circumstances change, the predictability of human behaviour is one of the most reliable constants in our economic environment. . . . It is the lack of preparation for change, the anti-change mechanism which is part of the human psyche, that ensures booms and depressions will continue for as long as there are emotional development lags in our technological development.

(Beckman, 1963: 207)

The concept of objectives

Once the interpretative task statements are determined there remains the vital need to translate these into operational terms. Concrete action can only take place on an intelligent scale if individuals, groups of individuals, and so the organization as a whole know what to do. Knowing what to do is derived from knowing the outcomes or results intended. These outcomes or results are really changes of state which are the product of the work which is done. In a school, they are notably changes of knowledge, attitudes, skills and conduct in the pupils. To attain these changes one asks 'What is the object of the work that you are doing?' Hence, the term *objectives* is used for the achievement of desired changes of state in people or materials with which an organization is concerned.

An objective is an intention to effect a new state in oneself, other people, animals, plants or materials, revealing values, commitment and timescale

An objective may be conveyed by means of spoken or written communication, or remain tacit and subject to inference by others

An organizational or corporate objective is one which is agreed by two or more people who form the organization and allow their conduct respectively to be governed by it until it has been achieved

---

Objectives are very often *assumed* and *implicit*, but need to be *articulated* and made *explicit*. The logic of it is plain and incontrovertible. The school has a task. The school is an organization. Organizations need objectives to fulfil their tasks. Some expressions of the importance of having objectives are contained in Table 2.3 (Hicks 1972: 60).

The task of an organization receives concrete expression in the form of objectives. The *task* may be to all intents and purposes permanent – in education, for example, it might be rather vaguely 'to provide an education for children'. *Objectives*, in contrast, are precise but variable expressions of this task at any given point of time. They take into account the changing

Table 2.3 Importance of organizational objectives

Objectives serve as reference points for the efforts of the organization.

Objectives are necessary for coordinated effort.

For coordination, the first step is to state the objectives the organization desires to achieve.

The organization that wishes to compete effectively and grow must continually renew its objectives.

Organizational objectives are the ends towards which all organizational action is directed.

Objectives are prerequisite to determining effective policies, procedures, methods, strategies and rules.

Organizational objectives define the destination of the organization; they move forward as rapidly as they are approached or attained.

Clearly defined organizational objectives are analogous to a star which can be used for navigation by ships and airplanes.

---

circumstances and capacity of the school as it seeks to fulfil its task. An organization needs objectives to get the best possible results, which are constantly elusive since the ability to supply 'good products' in education, as in manufacturing, is by definition never sufficient (Boulding 1953).

In simple terms, as objectives are reached new ones need to be set or existing ones reiterated if they are still appropriate. Reality, however, is more complex than this suggests. In practice, at any one point of time, many objectives are in the act of being realized, others are on the way to being realized and in the case of yet others little or nothing may have been done towards their realization. Hicks (1972) depicts these three kinds respectively as immediate objectives, attainable (i.e. probable) objectives and visionary (i.e. possible) objectives. Today's immediate objectives were yesterday's attainable objectives being formulated, and today's attainable objectives were yesterday's visionary objectives being thought about.

> Objectives define the destination of the organization; they should be reiterated or modified as soon as they are attained

All objectives, and the synonyms used for this term, envisage a desirable outcome of some kind as a result of cooperative action. Objectives are desired changes of state in people or in materials which will be brought about by the action of the organization and without which they would not occur. In schools it is necessary to take into account three categories of objectives: personal objectives; educational objectives; and resource objectives.

Personal objectives

Personal objectives are those formulated by teachers or pupils or other members of the organization. Such objectives foreshadow changes which people wish to achieve in themselves, in others, in working conditions and in their terms of employment.

It is important for individuals to have personal objectives. It is important that they should be able to modify them in the interests of themselves and the community as a whole. The question of personal objectives, therefore, has an educational aspect as far as the school is concerned.

> ... the choice of objectives can be a matter of life and death, either for a business or an individual person. In recent times several large and highly regarded businesses have accidentally destroyed themselves by pursuing objectives beyond their capabilities, not realizing that they had insufficient financial or technical strength. On the other hand, many other businesses, by modernizing their objectives and making them compatible with current market conditions, have revitalized themselves, rising out of a state of weakness and decay into a new period of growth. So it has been also with individual men and women, some of whom have damaged their lives and happiness by over-rigid adherence to inappropriate personal objectives, whereas others have found contentment or perhaps new inspiration by throwing away old objectives which were unobtainable and taking up more realistic ones better matched to their abilities and circumstances.
>
> (Jackson 1975:245)

It has not always been viewed as appropriate to consider personal objectives in the context of organization studies and to take them into account as an aspect of management. At one time, industrial practices and social values assumed a harsher separation of the interest of the organization as a whole and those of any individual member. The contract of employment in effect was based on the exchange of selective factors. In more recent times the psychological factor has been given more recognition. This movement has had its expression in the changing general climate of interpersonal relations and differences of social distance in organizations.

The recognition that personal objectives exist does not necessarily lead to attempts to take account of them in organizations. Personal objectives are based on different values but, 'all decisions are based on values ... two individuals faced with a similar choice may make very different decisions, both of which are equally valid in terms of their own value-systems' (Watts 1974:48). The magnitude of the task of decision-making in schools which actually attempted to take account of personal objectives which are so inevitably as diverse, if not mutually contradictory, as they are voluminous, is self-evident. This partly explains why teachers have traditionally been expected to subordinate their own personal objectives to the common good of the school. As has been described by Watts (1976:129–30) in the case of secondary schools, and Donaldson (1970) in the case of primary schools, the common good has often been defined by the head.

The current widespread practice of consultation and use of participative strategies in the management of a school may involve considerable strength of purpose as far as the head of school is concerned. Given the diversity and volume of personal objectives involved, it always represents a more arduous, time-consuming and potentially risky strategy for managing. With reference to the personal objectives of *new* teachers in the school, it is not long before they discover that their responsibilities go materially beyond actual classroom teaching. Teachers find that they are not free to initiate all they had intended – for purely organizational reasons. They then become determined to find the means to unlock the organizational doors to reach the educational and professional goals they have chosen, or else suffer discouragement and loss of morale as part of the process of reconciling their own personal objectives with those of others.

In the case of pupils, the fact that school makes a difference to personal objectives has been re-established (Rutter *et al.* 1979) in the face of scepticism (Coleman 1966; Jencks *et al.* 1973). The fact that pupils have personal objectives at all needs no elaboration. Often they nicely coincide with what the school seeks, but only too often may be perceived as against the interests of the school, extending to the encouragement of disaffection in others or the outright obstruction of learning activities. The difficulty of reconciling in the same school diverse personal objectives is all too clear. The head of a primary school made this point succinctly:

> On the same morning recently I saw two sets of parents. One pair was totally concerned with the academic progress of their child. The other was totally preoccupied with the social and emotional aspects of their child's experience in the school. Any suggestions I made to the one pair that there were other matters to be concerned about as well as academic performance fell on deaf ears, as did reverse suggestions in the case of the other pair.

Personal objectives are concerned with desired changes in oneself and others, and in conditions of work and terms of employment

---

Educational objectives

Educational objectives are concerned with the changes of state sought exclusively in people. They are changes of behaviour consisting of changes in knowledge, attitudes and skills. They may include those which do not affect others – for example, habits of study – and those which directly affect others, such as the tolerant treatment of the weak. Changes of state in all cases may involve unlearning as well as new learning. In the context of schools, educational objectives are concerned with changes of behaviour in the *pupil*. This usually means changes imposed or engineered but might equally be those defined by the pupil for himself.

There is no shortage of discussion at various levels of abstraction on the task which the school as an organization has or should adopt. All of the examples from prescriptive philosophy inevitably embody a decided outlook, a balanced judgement or a pronounced bias, according to taste (Nash *et al.* 1967). The school faces the forbidding problem of converting such task statements into practical steps (Ashton *et al.* 1975). Critics argue that the relationship between the declared task and organizational achievement is incongruous: 'Institutional goals continuously contradict institutional products' (Illich 1973:111). This would be quite apparent if the task of the school was seriously to be regarded as 'inevitably to some extent a tug-of-war between the corrupting values of adult society and the efforts of teachers to help children to withstand them' (Clegg 1974).

The *social utility* theme accounts for many prescriptions and is based on the acquisition by the pupil of cognitive, communicative, adaptive, judgemental and creative skills. A strong emphasis on the future-orientated nature of the task appears in the assertion that everywhere there is an insistence 'on the supreme need to teach pupils how to adapt themselves to various requirements, on the need to provide them with a basic education broad enough, and a way of thinking general enough and leave them equipped to acquire later any specialized knowledge which they may need' (Reuchlin 1964:32).

Some prescriptions have stressed the multi-dimensional nature of the task of the school as an organization. It has been seen to consist of facilitating literacy and preparation for working life, providing a 'social adjustment' centre, acting as an agent of social change, encouraging divergent thinking for social modification, offering welfare services and job training (Koerner 1968).

The rights of the individual pupil concerned and the qualitative aspect of scholastic experiences are expanded in other prescriptions. For example, ' "education" implies the transmission of what is worth-while to those who become committed to it ... must involve knowledge and understanding and some kind of cognitive perspective, which are not inert [and] at least rules out some procedures of transmission on the grounds that they lack wittingness and voluntariness' (Peters 1966:45).

A position for the existential aspect of the task has also been claimed. If the organization exists to provide information which is essential to the business of living and to inculcate valuable skills then it should also contribute to the spiritual development of the individual (James 1949). This has been delineated as follows. The individual on leaving the organization should:

- have acquired knowledge relevant to the solution of problems
- [be] capable of choice and self-direction
- [be] able to initiate action and be responsible for it
- learn critically and [be able to] evaluate the work of others
- [be able to] adapt to new problems
- [be able to] cooperate with others. (Sim 1970:59)

The tendency to expect too much of the school, however, has been tempered by timely reminders of the practical limits (Tyler 1967), but large demands continue to be made, as follows: 'If our educational philosophy accepts individual responsibility, not social guilt, as the final determinant of conduct, then we shall see some remarkable changes in the curriculum' (Ardrey 1972:340).

It is tempting to cling to conventional notions of task and to avoid any attempt to reconceive the objective on grounds of being unable to meet inordinate demands. In the future, it seems that the school's task may be seen as part of a new social strategy, which involves the substantial reappraisal of the requirements of a large range of organizations. 'The normal period of schooling is insufficient to create the understanding and moral sense necessary . . . The need for a fully developed civic sense is now more urgent than at any time in history. Industry and commerce must see themselves as largely responsible for the further development of this sense beyond what can possibly be done in the schools' (Lyons 1971:213).

It is evident from this selection of comments that different spokesmen for the community define the task of the school in various ways. These are sometimes mutually contradictory and often ambiguous, leaving plenty of scope for the school to choose its own ground. This involves choosing the prime values and order of priorities that will characterize its educational objectives. In this connection, the introduction of the National Curriculum has been of historic importance because for the first time the school has been presented with a curriculum content tied to specific objectives, as a statutory requirement in the public sector. This is not to say, however, that they inevitably constitute a school's sole educational objectives – perhaps far from it. Beyond meeting the requirements of the National Curriculum the school is still free to have additional educational objectives which can give a particular school its own stamp and its pupils a distinctive blend of knowledge, attitudes and conduct.

An important implication of this is that the compelling pressure on the management of the school to meet the minimum objectives of the National

Curriculum provides new ground for the assessment of staff performance. The central drive of the school is likely to be towards achieving ever improved performances in terms of these objectives, as has previously been the case in senior secondary schools over public examination results. Those members of staff who most facilitate the realization of the performance levels the school seeks are most likely to be favourably appraised in formal and informal ways by their peers and superordinates. Any system of staff appraisal and programme of staff development may be dominated by and cast in terms of the precise contribution made by particular members of staff to the collective and inescapable obligation posed by the National Curriculum.

> Educational objectives are concerned with changes of behaviour in the pupil in terms of his or her knowledge, attitudes and skills

Resource objectives

The word 'resources' in teaching is used in two ways. In common use it is given a narrow meaning, referring to the physical materials and equipment which the teacher needs either to make his teaching possible or to enable the pupils to do their work or both. Typically, teachers speak of 'audio-visual' resources such as cassette recorders, overhead projectors, video machines, computers and cameras, as well as a whole array of reprographic machines as their 'resources'. Such resources have transformed a great deal of teaching and learning activity in schools, giving rise to such concepts as 'resource-based learning', 'individualized teaching', 'programmed learning' and 'library resource centres'.

A management perspective in teaching, however, needs to give the word 'resources' an *inclusive* meaning. Resources are everything at the school's actual or potential disposal to enable it to reach its objectives. This meaning of the word was behind the attempt by the former Council for Educational Technology to identify 'the main factors which appear to produce successful resource organization; that is, the effective and efficient use of all available resources, whether books, film, videotape, OHP transparencies, space, money, staff or equipment, to support a curriculum designed to meet the needs of the school' (Thornbury *et al.* 1979:11).

Resource objectives, therefore, are concerned with changes of state in the human and physical resources which are or could be available to the organization to fulfil personal and educational objectives and to discharge the task of the school. They are concerned with the current use of staff, time, space, equipment, materials and money, the quantitative and qualitative changes which might be made in them and the future uses to which they might be put. They are also concerned with internal procedures, rules and regulations, the climate of working conditions, and not least the external relations which give the school as an organization its professional and public image. Resource objectives should be highly sensitive to the ever-changing conditions of life inside and outside the school.

> Resource objectives are concerned with changes of state in both internal and external resources which may be used to realize the school's educational objectives and as many personal objectives as possible

The need is to marshal resources in the best combination possible to suit the interests of the particular school. This is the basis for the policy of granting financial autonomy to the school, generally known as local financial management. With extended powers of virement a school can interchange its resources at its own discretion. For example, it may prefer to have more equipment rather than an additional member of staff.

Schools in the public sector of education are therefore now less subject to the direction of their local education authority with regard to the kind and volume of resources they may use. Once the overall financial grant is made, the school can exercise its own judgement over how it is used. Schools in the independent sector must in contrast first find their own income from fees and other sources. The risks involved for each kind of school are self-evident. In the public sector at least there must be enough financial acumen and managerial ability to make do successfully with what is granted. In the independent sector in addition there must be the strategic ability and drive to generate the necessary income and balance it with expenditure needs. As with businesses in times of recession, an independent school may manage its financial affairs badly and be forced into desperate appeals for temporary support – such as to parents and alumni – to survive.

There is a special onus on schools in the public sector in that the expenditure of public funds must demonstrably be efficient. This applies equally to the school which remains under the local education authority but with local financial management and to the school which opts out of the control of the local education authority in favour of direct funding from national government.

> Organizational objectives for a school consist of
> - personal objectives
> - educational objectives
> - resource objectives

Table 2.4 Educational objectives for deriving resource objectives

1. To be able to write a short letter to a friend or relation.
2. To be able to write a simple short story.
3. To know and occasionally read from the local paper and a daily paper.
4. To be able to use a public library alone.
5. To be able to go into the nearest large town alone.
6. To be able to find the way around a large building.
7. To be able to start a conversation with an unknown adult.
8. To be able to remember people's names.
9. To know the local area, roads, villages and suburbs by name.
10. To be able to work a tape recorder, slide projector, camera, record player and to know the difference between battery and mains power.
11. To have used simple tools: saw, chisel, hammer, screwdriver.
12. To be able to write legibly in a joined hand for note-taking.
13. To be able to look up words in a dictionary and to use the index in a reference book or an atlas.
14. To know the four rules in arithmetic and what processes are meant by signs for addition, subtraction, multiplication and division.
15. To be able to multiply and divide numbers up to 100. Five times eight equals forty, forty divided by five equals eight.
16. To work unsupervised for an hour.
17. To be prepared to accept more distant and formal relationships with several teachers rather than an intimate relationship with one.
18. To be prepared to take part in more outdoor games and to use gym equipment, to change properly and to take showers.
19. To be prepared to be separated from close friends who may be put into other classes.
20. Remember to accept the complete change of status from being in the oldest group at the primary school to becoming 'a little 'un' at the secondary.

Source: C. Jarman: 1977, 5

Critical aspects of objectives

There is a critical difference between educational objectives and resource objectives. By their very nature, educational objectives are infinite in that we want the best for our children. We are reluctant to exclude any desirable outcome and therefore to assign priorities. Resources are, however, by definition limited. Resource objectives, therefore, must of necessity be finite. The assignment of priorities in the realm of educational objectives is of the utmost importance. It is difficult to establish such priorities but to do so is a central responsibility of school management. Furthermore, educational objectives must be systematically translated into a form which can be used as a precise reference for the deployment and development of resources.

Table 2.4 shows a set of clear statements of the skills which pupils are expected to have on leaving a particular school. It was compiled before the advent of the National Curriculum and illustrates how the scope of educational objectives can go beyond the purely cognitive and manipulative to the relational, attitudinal and emotional realms. The list drawn up is not in any order of priority. Nevertheless, it represents a sufficiently limited and precise set of changes in the pupil which a school may wish to achieve, and provides a very useful measure for the disposal of the organization's resources.

With the establishment of the National Curriculum it is tempting for schools to regard their educational objectives as synonymous with the targets that come with the compulsory curriculum – at least insofar as *explicit* educational objectives are concerned. Almost certainly every school has *implicit* educational objectives over and beyond those of the National Curriculum. It is probably the best practice to set the sights of the school in terms of its educational objectives at a level which includes the targets of the National Curriculum as an integral and important part but which is by no means the whole of it.

It is self-evident that objectives and resources must match. In other words it is unreasonable to set objectives which lie beyond the human capacities and the physical means which the organization commands. Conversely, it would be reprehensible to set objectives that were well within the potential of the resources at the disposal of the organization. If the one is demoralizing for organization members, the other is wasteful and frustrating. Both are species of bad management since the idea of management is to get the very best out of all the resources available. The ideal is an optimum match between objectives and resources, even when conditions are antipathetic. *Good management is that which obtains exceptional results with unexceptional resources in unpropitious circumstances.*

All the activities of the school as an organization should relate logically and exclusively to the set of educational objectives which has been adopted. The realization of objectives which stretch resources to the full must be the central measure of organizational effectiveness and managerial competence. From this it follows that all identifiable sub-parts of the organization such as departments, upper, middle or lower school, teams, houses, year groups or classes should have their respective objectives. These should show how each part is contributing to the educational objectives of the school.

> The coordination of objectives is necessary for organizational effectiveness

Ultimately, the objectives defined by each teacher for a given period – an hour, a week, a term – should indicate the small steps by which the larger behavioural changes sought in the pupil may be achieved. In

principle it is important to do this: in practice it is difficult to do so. '...
complexity of organisation ... makes it more difficult for teachers to
coordinate the learning of the pupils, to plan and consult together and to
attain a synoptic view of the curriculum offered by the school and of their
contribution within it' (Department of Education and Science
1979:260–1).

Nevertheless, the need to do it underlies the various efforts made by
schools to overcome the difficulties. Some schools make an appointment
of a member of staff to coordinate the curriculum as a specialist
responsibility, while some large schools may have an interlocking committee system.

If the school were completely rational as an organization, even the
personal objectives of each individual member would relate logically and
exclusively to its educational objectives but in practice a great deal of
variation exists. In every school the personal objectives of a particular
teacher or pupil will be in part or wholly eccentric, deviant and even
hostile to the declared educational objectives. Whilst the ambivalence or
dissent of individuals can be accommodated, the complete secession of a
formally constituted part of the organization such as a team or department cannot be permitted. At least, it cannot be permitted until and
unless the educational and or the resource objectives have been modified
to take account of the departure which the group concerned wishes to
take. An example of this would be the case of a school which had
adopted a mixed ability teaching group policy throughout. Individual
teachers might deviate from this principle in their classes and be
tolerated. Whole teams or departments on the other hand would have to
work for and wait until the larger principle of team or departmental
autonomy was established before they could practise their preferred form
of pupil grouping. Their choice of practice would by then have been
legitimized by the considered modifications to the school's education and
resource objectives.

The time-scale for setting objectives must inevitably reflect the work
cycle of the organization concerned. Critical factors determine these times
in every case. Just as in agriculture one of the factors will be the seasonal
cycle so in a school the factors will include, for example, population size
and mobility, the development of the local community, the teacher supply
cycle, the external examination cycle, the period of time spent by the pupil
in the school, and, above all, the growth and development of pupils in
relation to the learning process.

From a consideration of all such factors, a school may set its overall
objectives in relation to the short, medium and long terms – respectively
called immediate, attainable and visionary objectives by Hicks (1972). An
example might be as follows:

Short-term: viability for the current school year
Medium-term: provision of progressive programme for the duration of
  a pupil's stay in the school
Long-term: enrichment of the local community.

Within each of these overarching categories more specific objectives may be identified to give greater guidance for action in each curriculum area. For example, in the case of Craft, Design and Technology (CDT) these might be:

Short-term: hire a new teacher for CDT work or encourage an
  existing member of staff to retrain
Medium-term: build an innovative CDT programme into the
  curriculum.
Long-term: provide CDT facilities and instruction for adults and youth
  groups in the community.

Thus far, school level objectives have been matched by curriculum objectives. Finally, however, there is the all-important need for operational or teaching objectives at the stage of implementation. These are concerned with the actual activities which people will undertake as a learning experience, chosen to produce changes in knowledge, attitudes and skills. For this reason they are often called 'behavioural objectives'. In the case of the example used – CDT – those involved would ultimately be exposed to a particular range of experiences in such activities as designing, sanding, sawing, joining and the like. Both qualitative and quantitative aspects would be taken into account when the objectives for each session were set.

If more precision can be built into objectives, however, the organization's members are able to direct their activities more constructively. Success or failure is correspondingly clearer but the consequences of this for both good and ill need to be taken into account. A sample list of the kind of items which might appear in the objectives of a secondary school is as follows:

By the end of (e.g.) the next academic year, it is intended to achieve the following objectives. These are listed under appropriate sub-headings:

School climate or morale
50 per cent reduction in absentee rates for pupils and staff
50 per cent reduction in accident rates
Extra-mural
20 per cent increase in attendance at school clubs
Establishment of two additional clubs
Curricular
Introduction of a new English programme for first-year pupils

Implementation of a revised Mathematics programme for third-year pupils
10 per cent increase in external examination passes
20 per cent improvement in all science attainment targets.

Strategies for formulating objectives

In the constant effort needed to develop and retain as much organizational unity as possible, the way in which objectives are formulated and adopted is of crucial importance. This applies particularly to educational objectives but may also apply to resource objectives.

Two general strategies are open to the school as an organization to achieve, maintain and modify its objectives. The 'top down' strategy is essentially *prescriptive* in nature. Objectives in this case emanate from a single individual – characteristically the head of school – or a very small group of senior staff. By a hard process of telling and directives or the softer process of selling and consultations, each sub-group and finally each individual is obliged or is persuaded to adopt them.

Quite apart from the sense of power and control which individuals may feel when they exercise this particular strategy, there are certain circumstances in which it is prudent to use it. In some organizations highly complicated and even dangerous technology is in use. At certain times organizations experience high staff turnover rates. Many organizations are subject to direct orders from 'parent' organizations. These cases certainly occur in commerce and manufacturing, and in all of them it can be argued that the 'top down' strategy is not only best but inevitable. Schools are also organizations which are subject to other organizations, such as local or central government agencies. In Britain prescriptions to schools from other organizations – in comparison with the practice in many other countries – are still on a limited scale but have increased with the introduction of the National Curriculum.

The 'bottom up' strategy is *derivative* in nature. Objectives in this case are articulated and refined by a process which begins with the personal objectives of individual members. It continues at the levels of persuasion and compromise when working groups within the organization – such as teams or departments in schools – arrive at a collective view. All such views are then synthesized and negotiated to form a set of objectives for the organization as a whole. This strategy, therefore, formally takes account of the interests of everyone and seeks to express objectives in terms of the wishes and perceptions of the current membership of the organization.

Objectives may be formulated by either a 'top down' or a 'bottom up' strategy

Just as the 'top down' strategy may please the organization's clients or owners at the risk of alienating its members, so the 'bottom up' strategy may cause the reverse. This can be illustrated in the school. Parents or the local education authority may be comforted to know that certain objectives are being adopted by the school, even though staff and pupils are not in sympathy with them. Conversely, the pupils and teachers of a school may be agreed in the adoption of objectives which parents and other external agencies regard as unwelcome. In practice, therefore, whichever strategy is adopted, the management of the school becomes involved in a process of reconciliation. The extent to which this is necessary depends upon the degree of discretion which the school enjoys in securing and deploying its resources.

A teacher in a position of managerial responsibility must be able to develop attitudes and skills which are appropriate to either the 'top down' or the 'bottom up' strategy. The individual's temperament may predispose him more readily to the one rather than the other. The differences between the two are quite pronounced as described in the following quotation which refers to the practice of implementing a 'bottom up' strategy by an individual manager.

> Far from being a man charged with the responsibility of creating policy, he finds himself obliged to feed in ideas (if he has any) at the level of departments or faculties, and then patiently to watch them from the chair at numerous committees, percolating upwards ... A large proportion of his time, and the bulk of his reserves of moral stamina, are spent in persuading committees of the virtues of unanimity, guiding ideas from one committee to the next, and concentrating ideas into forms which admit of administrative action ...
>
> (Ashby 1966)

For a variety of reasons, the advocacy if not the practice of a 'bottom up' strategy is now in vogue. In the European Community, ideas of industrial and social democracy, 'job enrichment' and participation may be viewed as part of a massive adaptation to the social demands of prolonged peace, technological innovation, less labour-intensive production and higher educational levels. Schools are expected to alert young people to changing values and behavioural norms. It seems that they may be invited to practise what they also present as precepts.

To illustrate the kind of event that a school would formally need to encourage if it overtly adopted a 'bottom up' strategy, the following example from French education is given. It is a copy of a document circulated to relevant parents in a school district originating among parents, pupils or others outside of the school.

The teaching of Arabic to immigrant children

In the minds of many of us, Arabic is not only a language. Arabic is a means of reading and understanding the Koran and of practising our religion better. In actual fact, the whole world recognizes Arabic as a language of great culture and of a brilliant civilization.

On the other hand, Arabic countries themselves, at international level, impose Arabic as a modern language and as a working tool in big international meetings . . .

For us immigrants, it's a necessity and a right to learn our language.

Do you know that your children can learn Arabic in school? They can choose Arabic as a first modern language from the first form of secondary school. So get together and make the request for it to the head of the secondary school which your child attends.

The minimum number of pupils necessary for a language class is 10. It is equally possible to group pupils from different classes or schools. At the moment in St Etienne, St Chamond and Chambon, Arabic is already taught as a modern language in certain schools.

If your children are at the primary school the circular of 1970, one of 1973, and another of April, 1975 provide for the organization of lessons in the mother language of the children . . . within school hours. In practice these are parallel classes, which mean outside normal classes and therefore in addition to them, and this causes problems. These lessons are only organized at your request.

Get together, organize yourselves and make joint requests to the local education authority, the heads of schools, and parents' associations.

A strong case can be made for expecting both strategies to be in formal use in a well-run school. The justification for this is the difference between educational objectives and resource objectives. Since educational objectives essentially concern the life chances of the pupil and the interests of parents and others in the community, a bottom up strategy in the age of the consumer society is the inevitable choice. The National Curriculum represents a consensus in this respect with regard to academic matters and is common to all schools in the public sector. Each school is then left to build up additional educational objectives of its own by a bottom up strategy.

Resource objectives on the other hand are the subject of managerial competence. Once the educational objectives are determined it is in the professional sphere of the providers – specifically the governors and teaching staff to deliver the product. The deployment of resources becomes a technical matter, at least for the most part. A top down strategy for resource objectives is more likely to be the case and appropriately so.

Educational objectives should be formulated by a 'bottom up'
strategy
Resource objectives are commonly formulated by a 'top down'
strategy, but may be formulated by a 'bottom up' strategy

The two strategies depicted here as 'top down' and 'bottom up' are
pure models. In practice the process of arriving at decisions over objectives
is usually a mixture of the two. Arriving at decisions is both an emotional
and a contractual process involving procedures which go in both directions
– 'down' and 'up' – to the extent of their becoming intermixed and
confused. This process often arouses anxieties and frustration, calling for
firm control and some precision. But it is still a psychological phase and it
may not be possible to avoid seeing it as a muddle. It can be characteristically like this in contrast to the actual implementation of decisions which
should be and can be orderly and systematically directed to the fulfilment
of the objectives concerned.

The reformed powers and duties of school governing bodies mean that
the governing body of a school as its 'board of directors' is an integral part
of the school's management structure. It is on the inside of the school
rather than an appendage as previously. Those who occupy the chairs of
governing bodies themselves will want to consider whether to adopt a 'top
down' or 'bottom up' strategy for the deliberations of the governors. In
turn the governors need to consider their own strategy as a body in
relation to the teaching staff of the school. The head has a crucial part to
play on both counts. There are certain to be occasions and issues which
invite the one and those which invite the other. In formulating objectives
and then setting out to fulfil them in reality, both the governors and the
teaching staff in their respective spheres need to be brought together and
involved in such a way that all their combined talents, ideas, knowledge,
enthusiasm and energies are evoked and employed for the good of the
school.

Organization exists when two or more people share a common purpose.
It persists as long as the common purpose is retained. The common
purpose may be viewed as the organization's task or reason for being in
existence. When many people are involved as members of an organization
it becomes difficult to obtain and retain such common purpose. Vague or
highly generalized definitions of common purpose mask this difficulty in
practice.

The main task of management is to ensure that all resources are used
to the full. In particular, those who manage in schools should try to reduce
the expenditure of time and energy of the members on organization
maintenance and organization defence costs, in favour of the education of

the pupils. Educational and resource objectives should be established and reconciled with personal objectives as far as possible to achieve results that are acceptable.

Acceptable results in themselves vary according to a number of different standpoints since schools are complex organizations in that there are several parties to the educational contract. Agreement on objectives – which implies agreement on the task of the school – is not easy to achieve. Two means for arriving at agreed objectives may be described respectively as 'top down' and 'bottom up' strategies. It is the vital job of management in the school to work towards unity, which may derive inevitably from the employment of both strategies according to circumstances and the particular objectives in question.

3   Technical skills in schools

If a number of people come together to form an organization, as in the case of the teaching and non-teaching staff of a school, there must be an avowed and agreed purpose, depicted as an organizational task. To be able to fulfil its purpose, to discharge its task, to reach its objectives an organization must have a technology. This is a word which has achieved common currency. It appears in everyday language for purposes of both public and private discussion. It punctuates reported or live debates in the mass media – whether of proceedings in parliament or of developments in particular industries.

In general the word stands for 'know-how' or the practical application of accumulated knowledge. People organized for work must follow the recognized and necessary practices which the particular work in question entails. The technology of an organization, therefore, may be regarded as the characteristic way in which an organization goes about its work. The school, for example, must know how to group the children for different purposes, the various methods of teaching which can be employed and how to design and implement curricular programmes, brought together by using the considerable art and science known as 'timetabling', but in schools, a member of the teaching staff at both junior and senior levels of responsibility must synthesize his or her knowledge and skills – in the sense of knowing what to do – and all the attributes of personality. The use of the term 'skills' in this chapter does not imply a mechanistic approach to any responsibility and job of any member of the teaching staff of a school. It rather refers to certain precise aspects of job content. But the discharge of that job as a whole takes all that a teacher has to give. The result is a synergistic one of competence or incompetence.

Technology is very closely linked with objectives. Some organizations are predominantly concerned with 'adding value' to inanimate objects, as in manufacturing. Some are concerned with 'adding value' to people as in training or rehabilitation organizations of many kinds. Some involve few people but much material and equipment, as in highly automated oil-refining processes or in the chemical industry. Some involve many people but few materials, as in educational organizations such as schools.

In the case of a manufacturing organization it is easy to understand its technology as the sequence of physical techniques used on the materials involved. It is less easy to understand the concept of technology when applied to the school, since the identity of the 'materials involved' or 'workflow' is less clear. Even so, visitors to a range of different organizations such as an engineering factory, a hypermarket, a hospital and a school would expect to find differences of knowledge and behavioural competences required to be a member of these organizations.

> Technology is the organization's collective 'know-how', i.e. the practical application of accumulated knowledge and the characteristic way in which the organization acts upon its workflow

Implicit in the concept of technology is the need for control. The use of the word technology implies that those who are members of the organization, particularly those in the most senior positions within it need to exercise a range of technical skills so that they are not merely seen to be in *command* but are also in *control*. The technology employed is intended to produce an organization that is *under* control and not one that is *out* of control.

> Control is needed if objectives are to be reached

Some organizations employ means of production that are well understood and *certain* in nature and which also achieve clear and predictable results. Manufacturing organizations generally fall into this group. Others employ certain means but face *uncertain* outcomes, as in medical or military organizations. Yet others again employ uncertain means – as in commercial organizations which use advertising, surveys and impressionistic bases for decision – but may achieve certain outcomes in the sale of products. Schools, however, fall into a fourth category where both means and outcomes are uncertain in nature. The use of measures in education for any purpose is consequently difficult.

It is easier to measure 'quantity' than 'quality'. In education, however, the quality is generally thought to be of greater importance than quantity. The issue of measuring in education is controversial since it involves the possibility of comparison between pupils and schools and the principle of formal accountability for the teaching profession. It is also complex, since the reliability and validity of measures are always in question. Even if they were not, there would still be an ideological question as to whether or not output measurement *should* be applied.

The school is a difficult organization to handle, therefore, because its technology is so uncertain. Control is elusive. The ways and means which teachers use to achieve their objectives are uncertain. For example, the kind of pupil grouping adopted carries no guarantees. The properties of one kind of grouping as compared with another are not universally reliable and incontestable. The precise nature of the outcomes which are achieved in the pupil are similarly uncertain. Dealing with people who are exposed to a wide variety of learning programmes is a more uncertain business than dealing with physical objects and involves issues of far more fundamental importance. Teachers might wish sometimes that some of the uncertainty could be reduced, but are well aware that it is rooted in cherished values which actually seek to perpetuate uncertainty.

The singular difficulty involved in trying to conceptualize the technology of the school as an organization arises over the status of the pupil. Viewpoints vary between regarding pupils as the 'materials' which the organization works upon and regarding pupils as themselves being 'members' of the organization, with all the rights and obligations of membership implied in Chapter 2. Each viewpoint reflects distinctive values. Each implies different approaches to the organization of the school.

If the pupil is viewed as an 'object', then the work of the school may be conceived as acting on the pupil to achieve desired results. This is a matter of *operating on* nature, as a craftsman works upon a piece of raw leather to produce an object of worth, of use and of beauty. In this case the pupil could not be regarded as an organization member. The organization exists to work on the pupil. The membership of the organization would therefore be confined to the teaching and non-teaching staff, that is the adult population of the school. Imagery which regards pupils as 'objects' may be anathema to many people. Nevertheless, it helps to highlight some important considerations. Adults *know* more and must ensure that knowledge and 'know-how' is passed on to the succeeding generation. Adults have a right to expect of young people a degree of conformity and a measure of acceptance of whatever social arrangements already exist.

In contrast, the pupil may be regarded as a 'subject'. The school may then be conceived as acting with the pupil to obtain desired results. This is a matter of *cooperating with* nature, as a gardener provides the best environment he can for a particular seedling. What the seedling will become is already implicit but requires the right conditions to enable it to happen. In a sense the seedling responds only to what is best for it. When applied to the school, this imagery suggests that the pupil must have a substantial part in choosing the experiences that will facilitate his own development. In this case, therefore, the pupil could be regarded as an organization member, giving rise to the problem of reconciling the pupil's interest with the legitimate demands of the community. The extremes depicted by the imagery of raw leather and the seedling present stark alternatives. Each implies its own characteristic organization and management. In practice, however, teachers are unlikely to be exclusively orientated to the one or the other. Nevertheless, a contemporary restatement of this dilemma for the educator still poses the extremes, invites a choice and implies important consequential differences in the organization and management of the school.

There are those who take the view that it is not possible to affect the learning of individual pupils very much. The corollary of this view is that educational resources must primarily be spent on classifying pupils as soon as possible. The criteria used would explicitly reflect the predicted school performance levels anticipated for each pupil. Fixed or stable variables must of necessity be found for such a purpose. The process involved is one of 'discovering' talent rather than 'making' it. Genetic factors are recognized as being predominant over environmental ones in the creation and maintenance of individual differences. This would form the basis of a school's policy for the distribution and use of resources. Clearly, the greater the specificity and rigidity given to such a system the larger the potential number of pupils who would find their classification and status uncongenial. Negative or hostile attitudes against learning and the school as an institution may be increased. Thus, the texture of school life and the benefits to the community would be impaired.

On the other hand there are those who advocate the alternative strategy. The vicissitudes and pressures of contemporary life demand that pupils in school are exposed to a different approach. The task is to discover among the variables that govern learning in the school those that are subject to alteration. The object is to control these alterable variables so that the very best learning opportunity for both individual teachers and individual pupils may be provided. This is the critical factor for the determination of the organization of the school and its management, based on a fuller understanding from research of the nature of such variables, how they may be altered, and with what effects. Among the alterable variables preferred in contrast to non-alterable variables are 'time-on-task' rather than 'available time', 'cognitive entry' rather than, 'intelligence', 'formative' rather than 'summative' testing, 'teaching' rather than 'teachers', and 'home environment' rather than 'parental status' (Bloom 1980: 382:385).

It is clear that the school is not involved in changing the state of, and adding value to, *inanimate* objects, as in a manufacturing plant. It *is* concerned with the adjustment of interpersonal relationships, with influencing or modifying individual conduct and physical and mental conditions, and with arranging interpersonal transactions. In this the school shares much in common with other people-oriented organizations in law, religion, social services and commercial services. However, if the school's concern for *systematic* and *broad based* learning is taken into the reckoning, something of the distinctive character of the school as an organization begins to appear, as indicated in such statements as the following which schools make about their work:

> the school's influence . . . affects almost every aspect of a child's development . . .
> it is our hope and ambition to promote the all-round development of the child to his or her full potential
> academic excellence . . . effort in sport . . . and . . . the personal development of the pupil
> school as a place in which to grow as well as to learn.

The existence of such concerns as are represented in these quotations, however, does not make the school as an organization unique. Training and educational activities in many walks of life – and not least within the frontiers of industry – may have the same concerns for personal development and accelerated learning. To the extent that similar work is being undertaken in such organizations as well as the schools and other educational institutions, the technological characteristics in all of them are similar.

Beyond these considerations finally, however, lie residual factors which *do* give the school its unique flavour as an organization. Whether regarded as organization members or not, pupils are under compulsion to attend; they are economically dependent; their age-range is confined and does not overlap with that of the teachers; there is a very wide range of maturity and ability levels within a school; the custodial powers of the teachers are great; the discretionary powers of the pupil are small; pupils lack the civic rights in schools which adults command – though assumptions about this are changing. Above all, pupils are being exposed to formative influences which affect their future lives as a whole and are designed to do so; they express themselves by informal collective behaviour but lack direct, formal representative mechanisms such as the unionization of organization members in adult life.

Alternative approaches

In practice, certain key factors provide technology with a characteristic appearance. It all depends on the way people think about the work that they do and the way in which they go about it. In school, for example, a pupil may be thought of in isolation – as a single individual – or as a member of a group. The group may be the object of attention or it may be seen as a convenient assembly of individuals.

In studies of technology (e.g. Lockyer 1962) there are a number of concepts which bear examination for the purpose of highlighting the practices which are adopted in teaching. *Job production* is the term used when one unit of production is regarded as a complete operation, undertaken by an individual or group in its entirety. The human and non-human resources of an organization are accordingly deployed to work on one or more such units in parallel. The building of a bridge and the manufacture of a tailor-made suit are obvious examples of this principle at work. In the school, this principle would be exhibited if the content, quality, sequence and pace of learning were determined differently and specifically in the case of each individual pupil. It might also be exhibited, however, in the case of the teaching group which remained intact for all its studies throughout the required schooling period, as in some countries, or for its passage through a given school, as might apply in a British junior school class.

If the work of the school is conceived as a series of set stages in a set sequence, important consequences are evoked. *Batch production* is the term used when a number of production units are moved through such a set of stages together. All the items stay in one stage until all the work for that stage has been completed in the case of every item. Only then is the batch passed on to the next stage. If all the units cannot be worked on to the same extent simultaneously at each stage, a great deal of time will be lost. Production may be discontinuous and inefficient. Items as varied as garments and motor-car panels may be manufactured by this method. In education this principle commonly appears as classes, forms or year groups. Pupils are in a stage for a year during which a teacher or group of teachers make their contribution. According to the principle it must be assumed that each pupil has reached a necessary standard in a given stage in order to be able to profit from the succeeding stage. Those who reach such a standard first are held up – as in traditional class teaching, particularly if the syllabus is prescribed – until the others also reach it. The use of the year's time span is strictly irrelevant since the principle requires only that enough time is taken to complete the work in the case of every unit. When this is achieved the whole batch then moves on.

In contrast, the essential feature of *flow production* is the achievement of continuous and progressive production in which all units are moved independently through the succession of given stages. As soon as one stage has been completed a unit moves on to the next stage irrespective of all other units involved. In the school this principle would apply in the case of individual pupils who were enabled to follow a prescribed and sequential curricular programme as far and as fast as they wished without reference to the performance of their peers. The critical difference between the operation of this principle and that of job production is that in the former the pupil follows a programmed learning path, as the National Curriculum may require, whereas in the latter he or she follows an individually guided learning path.

Job production	– each item is an end in itself until all work on it is complete
Batch production	– each item awaits completion of work on all other items before the next stage is begun
Flow production	– continuous and progressive work on all units moving independently through the stages of production

These *modes* of working must not be confused with the *scale* of working. Mass production is not a further mode of production but simply indicates the scale of production. A school is not obliged to adopt any particular mode of production according to its size. Mass production is critical for its effect on *quality* of production. It implies *uniform* quality rather than, as is often inferred, *low* quality.

A further set of concepts formulated by Thompson (1967) also offer the teacher a technological framework. The term *long-linked* technology has been coined for any process which consists of a series of steps which must be taken in a fixed and inescapable sequence. In schools, for example, some curricular material – as in the fields of mathematics, the natural sciences and foreign languages – are well structured in nature. Pupils need to study them in an orderly sequence. The policy for grouping pupils for these subjects should, therefore, bear this in mind. A second term is that of *mediating* technology. Many schools regard the interpersonal networks made possible by different groupings of pupils as an educational factor in themselves. Pupils can learn from each other and help each other. Examples of this principle are vertical grouping policies in primary schools and integration policies of primary and secondary education in which the physically, emotionally or mentally handicapped have at least some educational experience alongside other pupils in the same classroom. Extra-mural activities of schools, such as visits for which instructors or guides are provided and family exchange programmes with foreign schools, also exhibit this principle. A third term is that of *intensive* technology. Resources are arranged in orderly fashion and made easily accessible. They remain uncommitted, however, until a demand is expressed. When this is articulated a precise package of responses is assembled which is specific to the need expressed. This could apply to teachers as well as materials and features in progressive education programmes which are determined by the interests and needs of each pupil, primarily mediated by his choices.

Long linked technology	– a fixed and inescapable sequence of steps
Mediating technology	– arranging transactions between those with a need and those with a means to satisfy it
Intensive technology	– resources are classified and banked, remaining uncommitted until a need is expressed

Personal skills

In working with pupils in the school, teaching staff and non-teaching staff apply a great deal of knowledge and use many skills which are commonly needed in a variety of different organizations. In addition, however, they need knowledge and skills which are more specific, if not unique, to schools as organizations. The technology of the school may, therefore, be said to have two aspects. One consists of *generic* skills, the other of *specific* skills.

Generic skills may be regarded as those which are common to all organizations because they are generated by the social values, approved practices and a general legal and economic framework which are common to those organizations. People are the bond which unites all organizations within the same community. The way in which they become prepared for and inducted into organizations, the terms and conditions of their employment, the treatment they receive from and give to others, and the levels of participation and job satisfaction which they experience, are all factors or variables in common with organizations. Experience gained in organizations other than schools can be of interest and use to those concerned with the management of schools. In turn, experience gained in the management of educational organizations can be of interest and use to those in other kinds of organizations. The stock of knowledge of organizations at large exists for the understanding and multifarious purposes of everyone.

Of paramount importance in every organization is the need to obtain, marshal and commit scarce resources together with the capacity for making the necessary decisions and the will to put those decisions into practice. Such decisions range from the trivial to the strategic and far-reaching. The capability which an organization possesses for doing this is vital to its success, to its ability to adapt to changing circumstances and so, perhaps to its very survival. Adequate decision-making processes are a necessity for the school as they are for any other organization. Such processes require a large range of often sophisticated human skills. These include the ability to conceive appropriate and effective processes in the first place, but also skills of implementation, maintenance and adaptation of such processes. Such skills are generic in that all schools and all types of organizations must have them.

Specific skills, in contrast, may be regarded as those which are required in one kind of organization rather than in another because of the singular differences in the work being undertaken. In practice, the dividing line between generic skills and specific skills is often blurred. Not all members of organizations possess specific skills. The possession of generic skills implies the possibility of easy transfer from one kind of organization to another. For example, a school secretary could easily be employed in another kind of organization, since shorthand and typing skills are sufficiently generic in nature. On the contrary, a teacher skilled in the diagnosis of reading difficulties and the teaching of reading could not readily transfer employment except to another school. The skills in this case are specific to the school as an organization. The same teacher, however, is exercising generic skills when chairing a meeting of colleagues, leading an investigation into an organizational problem or writing a report.

> Organization members must between them exhibit
> - generic skills – those that are common to all organizations, and
> - specific skills – those that are subject to special training or learning within a given organization and peculiar to it

If technology is the organization's collective 'know-how', the practical application of accumulated knowledge, the school can appear to be deceptively simple in nature. Visitors to some organizations may be immediately impressed with the visible sophistication and complexity of the technology needed. To the lay visitor a school may convey little at first sight, but evoke greater respect over a longer period. The 'production' process is slow and the time-cycle is long. The programme which a pupil actually experiences in school is the result of a great deal of knowledge and experience put to practical use by the teaching staff. It is, for example, a daunting and complex task to set out to teach and to get a wide range of pupils in a group to learn the skills and concepts in the following list – the sort of demand made under the National Curriculum, and standard to all schools.

Curiosity
Originality

Perseverence
Openmindedness
Self-criticism
Responsibility
Willingness to cooperate
Independence in thinking
Observing
Proposing enquiries
Experimenting/investigating
Communicating verbally
Communicating non-verbally
Finding patterns in observations
Critical reasoning
Applying learning
Concept of causality
Concept of measurement
Concept of volume
Concept of force
Concept of energy
Concept of change
Concept of interdependence
Concept of adaptation

The teacher, to achieve such learning objectives by means of chosen technology, seeks to control the *learning process* of the pupil. Conceived inclusively, this learning process has four dimensions:

1. Content of learning
2. Quality of learning
3. Sequence of learning
4. Pace of learning

Control over the learning process is ultimately obtained by affecting the pupil's self-control and by the way in which the resources of the school are deployed. A particular school's efforts in this direction will be determined by the combined operation of a number of factors. The basic values of its members will govern the organization's objectives and form of organizational communication. The knowledge which the members have of psychology will regulate the school's appreciation and understanding of individual differences. The knowledge which members have of sociology will determine its understanding of environmental influences, and their knowledge of social-psychology will determine the organization's ability to construct and manage groups. The professional background of the teaching staff – their training, experience and qualifications – modified by, and reflected in, the variable circumstances and practices peculiar to the particular school, complete the network of factors which act to produce a specific set of responses.

In practice, knowledge is used to make choices in a large number of decision areas. The following schedule has been advanced as a framework within which teachers make significant choices which control the content, quality, sequence and pace of the pupil's learning.

- Planning the nature of materials for study
- Specifying the method of studying the materials
- Deciding between self-pacing and group-pacing the materials for presentation
- Identifying the nature of the activities the learner is to engage in with respect to the materials, or the objectives
- Monitoring the learner's progress and taking corrective action
- Making explicit the role of the teacher in respect of materials and progress
- Scheduling group activities and the teaching methods to be employed
- Deciding the time limits and the allocation of plant and resources
- Assessing performance
- Providing counselling and guidance in cases where the learner is expected to share in the control as in options regarding ends or means.

(Gagné and Briggs 1979)

At the actual point of delivery, the concept of technology as applied knowledge or the characteristic way in which an organization acts upon its workflow is well illustrated in the case of the teacher. The following have been suggested as elements of the 'know-how' which teachers need. They are classified in two areas.

1. *The series of behavioural events which the teacher offers and regulates in stages*
   - Gaining attention
   - Informing the learner of the objective
   - Stimulating recall or prerequisite learning
   - Presenting the stimulus material
   - Providing learning guidance
   - Eliciting the performance
   - Providing feedback about performance correctness
   - Assessing the performance
   - Enhancing retention
   - Encouraging transfer of learning

(Gagné and Briggs 1979, ch. 9)

2. *The range of media by which the learning may be induced*
   - Direct, purposeful experience, e.g. experiment
   - Contrived experience, models; mock-ups; simulation
   - Dramatized experience – plays, puppets; role-playing
   - Demonstrations
   - Study trips
   - Exhibits
   - Educational television
   - Motion pictures
   - Still pictures
   - Radio and recordings
   - Visual and verbal symbols
        (Gagné and Briggs 1979:180–2: from E. A. Dale 1969)
   - Computers

Facing up to problems

The most important aspect of an organization's technology is the ability to solve problems at all levels. The distinctive characteristic of professional status is knowing what to think about and how to proceed when faced with unexpected or novel circumstances. Knowing how to carry on the work of the school on a directed or prescribed basis is a *reactive* capacity. Knowing how to cope with the inevitably novel patterns of circumstances, in order to maintain the work of the school at a high level of excellence, is a *proactive* capacity calling for a person who can seek out solutions by one method or another and anticipate events.

Various attempts have been made to analyse and describe all that is entailed in the behaviour of people who manage organizations successfully. In practice actual behaviour is never very tidy. Thus, all attempts to capture the spirit and many dimensions of behaviour involved in finding successful solutions to problems in the management of organizations must inevitably be inadequate in one way or another. Consequently, models based on accumulated experience are sometimes dismissed as 'mere theory'. It has been said, however, that there is nothing so practical as a good theory – if theory consists of making the past available to work for the future.

Three models are presented: they are identified respectively as the deterministic model; the probabilistic model; and the problem-solving model.

Deterministic model.   The deterministic approach relies upon objectivity, definable cause and effect and full control. The behavioural steps in this approach are as follows:

1. Formulate the problem on the basis of observation/information
2. Identify all the variables involved
3. List all possible solutions
4. Hold all variables constant except one
5. Apply the various solutions in turn
6. Record the range of results
7. Select the optimum result
8. Test in pilot project
9. Evaluate pilot project
10. Implement and maintain.

It is evident from what has been said previously in this chapter that this approach will have limited application in the school, given the high levels of uncertainty. Nevertheless, this approach can be applied to selected classes of events. All kinds of routine events which seek established procedures may be subjected to this approach. Examples of these are the ordering, storing and distribution of consumable stock, the use of equipment, the access of parents to the school and a pupil record system. In this approach one is looking for a specific answer to a specific problem, usually restricted to objective events.

> The deterministic or scientific approach is useful for understanding and finding solutions to specific and small-scale problems in schools, especially those involving routine events

Probabilistic model.   The major events which cause concern in schools, however, are of a more diffused and non-routine nature. They are mostly problems of relationships and arriving at a suitable curricular programme for young people who are passing through the school only once. The complexities introduced by uncertainty and temporariness require a wholeness of view in which disparate elements can be united and which has a dynamic or unfolding quality about it. The deterministic or scientific approach is inappropriate for this purpose. The probabilistic or systems approach is better adapted to provide insight and understanding.

In a systems approach uncertainty is assumed. All the people, events, procedures and processes of the school at any time are regarded as a whole or single 'system'. The school is part of a larger (education) system, consisting, for example, of all schools of the same type in the locality or region – in the same way that, for example, the motorway system is part of the national transportation system of rail, air, waterway and roadway services. The school itself as a system in its own right is made up of any number of identifiable 'sub-systems' that one wishes – just as in the case of a motor-car one can identify its electrical, petrol supply, suspension, heating, engine cooling and other sub-systems. The greater the number of viable sub-systems that can be identified the better.

The sub-systems of a school will vary in kind and should be intentionally disparate in nature. They might include organizational parts such as teaching staff as a whole, non-teaching staff as a whole, year groups of pupils, a teaching team or departmental staff. They might include programmes for special needs or for mathematics or reading throughout the school. They might also include less tangible factors such as staff morale, pupil discipline, staff development or the school's public relations.

A systems analysis, therefore, involves an identification of the following elements (Wyant 1971).

1. The system's boundaries
2. Its sub-systems
3. Relationships between the system and its sub-systems
4. The relative importance of each sub-system
5. The order and dependencies which exist among the sub-systems
6. How systems or sub-systems may be added or subtracted
7. How a system or sub-system may be amplified
8. How a system or sub-system provides feedback
9. How systems or sub-systems interact
10. The nature of the linkages between systems or sub-systems.

Systems thinking is an aid for dealing with the complex phenomena which make up organizational life. It provides no answers in itself. It provides no prescriptive solutions. It does, however, provide a means of clarification, a means of greater understanding and a more inclusive conceptualization in the expectation that better decisions and wiser judgements may thereby be made.

> The probabilistic or systems approach is useful for understanding and finding solutions to non-specific and large-scale problems in schools, especially those that involve non-routine events

Problem-solving model   This approach to handling organizational problems owes much to the strict discipline and sequential steps of the traditional scientific, deterministic model but is modified to suit more diffuse and intangible matters with which management is often concerned in addition to selective technical problems. It still consists of a set of logical steps with the whole emphasis placed on *method*. Information is continually important as is the classification of facts but in the end it is the methodical treatment of perceived realities which carries the manager through to applicable solutions, even though these in turn become bases for the creation of further problems. A term coined to describe the resolution of a problem in this way is '*satisficing*' rather than satisfying. Problems in organizational life can never be satisfied in the sense of achieving a full and final solution but only 'satisficed' in the sense of creating an interim state which is at least for the time being more acceptable to more people than the preceding state which acquired 'problem' status.

Stage 1 in the problem-solving cycle is to formulate the problem very clearly and precisely. This is an exhaustive exercise since it requires:

1. Adequate relevant information or evidence which must be sufficient in breadth and quantity to show a direction. It needs to be borne in mind that a single piece of evidence or one fact can be totally neutralized by another, so a larger body of facts or evidence from several sources is desirable.

2. A prior, honest understanding of and commitment to an objective, since a problem can most clearly be understood as an obstacle on the way to an objective. If there is no objective there is no problem because there can be no obstacle. But in practice, objectives commonly lack sharpness of definition. Consequently, problems are also too often dimly perceived – to the extent that objectives are unclear. Vague feelings of unease and random complaints substitute for the appreciation of the presence of a definite problem preventing the realization of a firm and clear objective.

Under such personal thought in the case of personal problems, or group discussion in the case of group problems, it may be concluded – once the objective is clarified and reiterated – that there is after all no problem.

The stage of formulation thus overlaps with that of Stage 2, which is interpreting the evidence once a problem has been diagnosed. This is to gauge the extent of the problem and what it means to the organization. It involves the discovery of reasons for the evidence or facts which are to hand, so it is a process of analysis followed by synthesis and full understanding. On this basis Stage 3 can then be entered. This consists of creating any number of means for correcting the unsatisfactory or unwanted state of affairs. This requires resourceful thinking and at this stage needs to be an exercise in unfettered thinking. The task at this stage is to make a list of all courses of action which can potentially apply to the perceived problem.

Stage 4 is that of decision-making, or choosing one of the many courses of action from the assembled alternatives. This process involves considerations of many kinds – legal, financial, cultural, social – and certainly those of morale and productivity. But over all presides psychological considerations with respect to the decision-makers themselves. The person or group making the decision is at the same time evaluating his or her or their own ability and willingness to be committed to the choice of alternatives made in the sense of carrying the decision through in practice. For example, the choice made may be seen to be a necessary but unpopular measure.

Stage 5 is practical action or the implementation of the decision. This is the stage of getting results and depends upon the will to succeed, persistence and hard work. It requires plans and preparations, and regulation and control, so that at the end of a prescribed and suitable period there can be a review and evaluation to see if the chosen course of action has been effective.

Problem-solving is the art of succeeding in difficult circumstances. It depends, in the first place, on understanding the essential nature of problems and on knowing how to think about them strategically. It is important to tackle problems in an orderly manner and to acquire *disciplined habits* of thought in solving them. Getting results has more to do with controlling one's own thoughts and action than with the overcoming of difficulties. It depends primarily on being conscious of the objectives that have been established and on being determined not to waste time and effort on those objectives which are known to be unimportant or of little value.

The concepts and precepts of the problem-solving model are sound enough to compel the attention of everyone with managerial responsibilities. They establish order out of muddle and have sufficient general applicability to daily life to warrant being a part of every child's and young person's education. Pupils can see an orderly and systematic methodology for dealing with complex human and material problems in school organization as well as being formally introduced to the principles and practice of problem-solving as part of the curriculum. Some of the topics in the latter case need to be as follows:

- What problems are and are not
- Where problems come from and how they show themselves
- How to make the best use of opportunities
- How to detect, identify and define problems
- How to increase one's understanding of a problem
- How to gather ideas and work out effective solutions
- How to choose which course of action to adopt and how to obtain commitment to it
- How to plan and control implementation so that we get the results we want
- How to assess results and learn as much as possible from experience.

(Jackson, 1975)

Management information

The solution of a problem at any level depends fundamentally on information just as the realization that a problem exists in the first place depends upon information getting to a point where its significance is appreciated. In a state of ignorance, not only may the solution to a problem never be found, the existence of the problem may never be known. A personal discipline of managerial behaviour therefore is openness to information whether pleasant or unpleasant, stretched to ensuring that adequate information is generated and flows to where it is wanted by appropriate means.

From the standpoint of organization and management, the ebb and flow of information may be conceived as a totality and made subject to study and understanding for practical, operational purposes. Information may be regarded as a single system because it is subject to increase, decrease, direction and application. It may be formal or informal. It can be formal because the generation, volume, flow, direction and use of it is deliberately organized. The formal system may also attempt to pre-empt, harness and use the informal system or 'grapevine' which exists in every organization. There is always the need for the manager to exercise skill in the gathering, analysis and use of available information for the good of the organization.

The argument for having a management information system generally relates to the essential management function of controlling the organization. Control in this sense is ensuring that the objectives set are actually reached. It can be justified in terms of the quantity and quality of the outcomes or results achieved as specified in those objectives. A management information system has two dimensions: *inflow* and *outflow*. The inflow provides management with information on which to base two kinds of decisions:

1. for taking corrective action immediately or in the short-term future
2. for reformulating objectives and devising a strategy to reach them in the medium- or long-term future.

The outflow provides management with the means to communicate chosen information to enable everyone concerned to sustain or take corrective action so that the objectives of the organization can be fulfilled.

Management information system, therefore, stands for the inclusive means by which what is happening, and how it is happening, both within the school, and in the relevant parts of its total environment, becomes known, distilled, stored as necessary and subsequently made available to those who need to have it in a form which will effect what should happen and how it should happen.

A system itself is subject to performance criteria. It is a serious matter if a system malfunctions. If this happens, interim crises appear but eventually the result may be a major impairment of the management's attempts to be effective. Consequently, a number of performance criteria need to be adopted and used to govern the design and functioning of the system chosen, however variegated its parts. These may include the following:

Inflow
- process without delay
- know the correct destination for action
- put into agreed form

Outflow
- put in explicit form
- give time for necessary action
- ensure fail/safe delivery

Both
- accuracy of information
- concisely presented
- quickly assimilable in form

A wide variety of information is needed, drawn from many zones and transmitted to many zones. A wide variety of means may be used. They should be suitable, efficient and effective. In essence they are few in number – by direct word of mouth or through an intermediary, on paper, by telephone or on tape. It is easy to be trapped into retaining conventional or habitual means when an alternative may be quicker, easier and cheaper.

Apart from the inflow and outflow dimensions, a system needs to be conceived from the standpoint of the sources of information it handles and the destinations for it. A classificatory scheme is necessary. Some sources and destinations are wholly confined within the school. Others cross into and out of the school. The information in total can be classified according to the groups of people involved, e.g. pupils, teachers, the media, parents and so on; or according to the nature of work of the school, e.g. subjects, supplies, security, supervision, pastoral and so on; or according to the school's management functions, e.g., the plant, facilities and equipment, staff, curriculum, finance and so on.

Information can never be complete, but what there is can at least be up to date. The axiom is to ensure the fullest possible information within the time available before action must be taken. On the inflow side the mechanisms may be too unwieldy or inefficient to serve management well at times. On the outflow side it is often the case that too little information is conveyed or that it is conveyed with too little time allowed for the action to be taken. Who should know and how much they should know are crucial issues. Selective amounts and destinations on the outflow side are probably inevitable and desirable.

The chief dangers can be as follows:

1. Having a lack of balance and differential efficiency and effectiveness between the *inflow* and the *outflow*
2. Having a system which is over elaborate for the information flow which it has to handle
3. Having a system which is overloaded
4. Having a system which is not checked from time to time with regard to recognized performance criteria.

The management information system exists for a purpose and should not exist for its own sake. The costs of maintaining it can exceed the benefits derived from it. It can become choked with inert if not useless information. These costs are measured in terms of time, storage space, retrieval difficulties and mounting preoccupation with processing information, especially through papers and meetings. The information required by management is primarily for the identification of actual or potential problems. It can be confined to the uses of a reactive management – information which shows that a problem already exists. It may constructively be used in the interests of a proactive management – to show that a problem is on its way with time to anticipate it. To this end, information entering the system should be sifted by its handlers for significance. Pettifogging detail needs to be avoided in favour of what is material to critical purposes and put in digested form. At all times and for all purposes a rule for written information could be that it should not exceed one side of A4 paper. Another could be that no-one should speak longer than three minutes in a meeting.

This is to suppose that a healthy climate exists in the school. A flow of candid information is required. People receiving and handling information can be tempted to stop it, filter it, or even twist or distort it to suit their own interests or to 'tell the boss only what they think he or she wants to hear'. Decisions can be made on the basis of wrong or inadequate information. Before a decision is made there should be a check on any vital information upon which it may depend. A good balance of soft means (hearsay, gossip, word of mouth, observation of incidents and knowledge of cases) and hard means (figures, written reports, surveys, models and precision data) needs to be developed for the generation and representation of information.

Teachers can be slapdash in their attitude to paperwork and have low levels of business competence. This may not be surprising in view of the basic preoccupation of the working day and pressures on non-teaching time from preparation and marking. But it may be surprising when the nature of the function of the school is considered and the example which should be set to children and young people. Everyone can begin to improve by giving attention to three things when engaged in talking about business matters and when writing about them; they are the ABC of management information systems

ACCURACY – BREVITY – CLARITY

Accuracy applies to the facts in the first place. But if information is relayed it should be finally checked before delivery – for example, *after* a paper has been typed. Brevity is a matter of grasping the essentials, making expert summaries and stating the essence of arguments. The key to brevity is knowing in the first place what one's interest is, what is at stake. In other words, where an objective exists it should be possible to recognize a threat to its fulfilment. The purpose of written material in a management information system is quite different from other uses with which teachers are constantly working in their educational task, notably the use of prose and the essay. Clarity is partly a matter of choice of words or figures but partly a matter of how they are laid out for speed of reading and ease of understanding. Models and diagrams or a few figures can save a lot of prose. These may be cultivated. Teachers could transfer skills already used in subject teaching or practise to extend their range of skills.

Information is conveyed by verbal or written means. It can be stored, if verbal on tape or if written, on paper or the word processor. In each the inflow and outflow dimensions of the system's many devices are used to aid efficiency and effectiveness. These range from the proforma to a regular meetings programme. It may be the case, however, that the management of the system is conceived in terms of each individual concerned. This is a *laissez-faire* approach which may not yield the results needed. Two steps may be taken to improve the management information system and business acumen of the school.

1. Appoint someone in a senior position to oversee the entire system. It should be part of his or her job description.
2. Hold periodic audits of the system (a) to modify it in the light of experience and (b) to make the staff member who is overseeing it accountable.

Inflow information can so easily be flawed or misleading. On taking up his appointment, the head of a secondary school reviewed the academic and behavioural standards, and work achievements of the pupils in the school. When sharing his reservations about his findings with his senior colleagues, he was assured by them that the school was doing just about as well as possible, considering the general calibre of the pupils. He was told that most of the children came from the huge council-house estate and that they were mostly disaffected and lacked support from their parents. Consequently, the new head was told that he should not expect too much from them. The head went away and analysed the pupil records. He calculated actual figures and armed with them invited his senior staff to tour the catchment area with him. They found that in fact only a minority came from the council-house estate. The majority came from a variety of other housing, including lower- and upper-middle-class districts. He concluded that ossification and low morale had set in, partly resulting from misinformation. He corrected the latter at once and successfully set about raising standards and achievements to higher levels.

The following is the substance of a view expressed by Michael Marland as Head of Westminster Community School, Paddington on Radio 4, November, 1986:

> Schools can be far too casual about the information they need before they take decisions and put those decisions into effect. Customarily they have been content to rely on non-quantitative data for the purpose. But for many purposes today a school needs to gather hard data. They should develop greater expertise in working with figures and learning how to present them as an integral part of their professional business.

It is a requirement of personal professional accountability for every individual to pause and consider from time to time what sort of performance he or she is achieving within the management information system. To evaluate this the following questions may be asked.

1. Is my in-tray ever empty? Is my out-tray ever full?
2. How well do I grasp essentials and stick to them in written papers?
3. Do I try to confine my telephone calls and conversations with colleagues to the business in hand?
4. Am I punctual for meetings and do I keep to deadlines?
5. Is accuracy a minor fetish with me?
6. Do I check information before I act?
7. When did I last pass on unsolicited information which I thought would be of interest to a senior colleague?
8. Do I make connections between seemingly disparate pieces of information?
9. Is my personal/office filing system effective?
10. Do I periodically audit the management information system or the part of it for which I have responsibility?

The need for management information systems and the volume and range of data which they carry are likely to increase. Machines will come to the aid of the school. Computers in administration are more commonplace. But above all, there is a need to develop the expertise of teaching staff in a field where there is some antipathy. A more businesslike attitude is needed to cope with the many items which now enter into the management information system, such as the following:

- the state of pupil profiles
- the establishment of staff appraisal and development programmes
- the extended involvement of parents
- the enlarged formal duties of the governors
- the progress of plans for curriculum development
- the mechanics and pressures of the National Curriculum
- the developing relationship between school and industry
- the increasing legal or quasi-legal specifications
- the need for public-image building and media links
- the state of the school's financial management.

> An effective two-way information system is vital for managerial control and organizational development

Financial skills

Of all the kinds of information in the system none is more important than financial information since all the activities of the school and its ultimate performance turn on soundly managed finances. The generation and flow of financial data are also important because of the need to compensate for the lack of financial experience and expertise which may be found among governors and teaching staff who in general have not been bred to financial management. Some schools may have a full-time specialist such as a bursar. Some may have a governor with professional experience in financial management such as banking. But in all cases adequate financial information within the general information system is needed to ensure control of expenditure and to ensure that the school as a whole and its various activities are economically viable.

The financial part of a management information system has three main sub-systems, each fulfilling a vital function.

1. *The Facilitative Function*   This sub-system is conceived as all that is required to collect and to secure monies from all sources, the mechanics of payments to all destinations, records of inventories, i.e. stored asset values, and the processes and procedures for establishing budgets and monitoring them.
2. *The Regulatory Function*   This sub-system is conceived as all that is

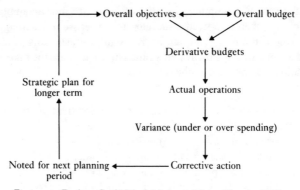

Figure 3.1 Budget Cycle Model (adapted from Young 1986)

required to have an overall picture of all transactions in relation to the general financial position as represented by the master budget. It is concerned with the school's main objectives and will therefore deal with projections, interim and final reports.

3. The Developmental Function   This sub-system is conceived as all that is required to make the best possible decisions about future courses of action. It provides cost information for any proposed purchase or expenditure, calculations of profitability or cost effectiveness of new projects, schemes, products or markets. Where uncertainty exists over the choice between real alternatives, it provides financial evaluations for the different plans and strategies under consideration.

In practice, these three main functions intermingle in nature and in time but may be represented in cyclical terms as in Figure 3.1 The first and founding stage is the interplay between the overall budget and the principal organizational objectives. Dependent or derivative budgets such as those for departments or other designated sub-units which are sometimes called 'financial' or 'profit' centres are formed eventually from this to identify the contribution of such sub-units to the whole.

With the practice of local financial management for all schools and financial independence from the local education authority perhaps for an increasing number of schools in future years, a financial culture needs to be prominent in school. It needs to be prominent but not dominant. It does not need to be dominant because the financial viability of the school does not depend upon the pupil as consumer, customer or client who pays directly for the services received at an economic rate. Pupils must attend school by law and there are purposes to be served beyond those of simple financial viability. Nevertheless, a new admixture in which financial awareness and expertise are added to the traditional cultural elements among all those responsible for the running of the school is needed. The financial element is a powerful future determinant and perspective. Even schools in the independent sector, however, fall short of having a full financial culture such as exists in manufacturing and commerce. Nevertheless, in schools as in all organizations general principles and many practices with respect to financial management apply with equal force. The chief concern is to remain solvent. Cash flow or liquidity – having enough ready money to pay one's way – is a manager's regular chief financial responsibility. The situation must not arise where so much cash is locked up in material, equipment, work in progress, finished goods and debtors that there is insufficient to meet urgent needs such as paying for vital supplies and services, and perhaps paying wages and salaries or meeting the claims of creditors. Financial management involves maintaining liquidity in the face of ever-changing conditions both on the supply side (income) and on the demand side (expenditure), whilst introducing one's own changes in objectives which of course may increase or decrease expenditure and as a consequence lead to moves to moderate income accordingly.

Budget management

Subject to the need to keep organization maintenance costs as low as possible, the budget is an indispensable tool of effective financial management. In schools it is a legal duty laid on the governors to ensure that a proper budget is prepared and agreed. This is for the school as a whole. There remains the question over how many derivative budgets may be necessary and how formal they need to be. Since the preparation and subsequent management of a budget is time consuming and therefore expensive, perhaps the watchword needs to be 'as few as possible'. A school with large sub-units such as departments is unable to avoid derivative budgets but they need to exist in a well-defined structure, avoiding overlap. Budget holders as individuals or groups need to have clear targets which become a subject for discussion at staff-appraisal time.

A budget-holder's share of the overall or master budget for the school can be determined in one of three ways. In the first case, some kind of standard costing or unit costing can be calculated. This may be, for example, the average cost per pupil per year from overall expenditure, yielding a per capita basis for a derivative budget. A second way is simply to repeat the previous year's sum, whatever the basis for it had been, but with an adjustment for inflation and/or a proportional adjustment up or down according to the overall figure available for the school as a whole. A third way is to assume a stand-still position in which there will be no expenditure. Each proposed expenditure is then treated on merit and must be independently justified. This way is usually known as zero-based budgeting and has the merit of enabling superordinate management to reward economies and prudent financial management in a subordinate or sub-unit and to punish profligacy and failure to reach objectives. It does however involve more work for the superordinate who must vet each proposed initiative either personally or through a committee.

Budget language will be a firmer feature of school discussion in the future than in the past. But it needs to be remembered that the use and success of a budget is having a happy and effective school. To this end a budget is the cause of meetings between staff and needs to generate cooperation and willing communication between them, applying to both horizontal and hierarchical relationships. Staff need to have detailed budgetary information at lower levels in the organization in such a way that they can identify with the school's overall objectives and feel that they are really contributing to them. Targets must be plain, realistic and achievable in the timescale provided. Feedback in the course of operations or during subsequent staff appraisal needs to be constructive. Interim or final reports of a budgetary nature need to be accurate, intelligible and closely relate in time with the events they portray.

Preparing budgets is a time-consuming task and often an irritant to teaching staff who want to devote their time to the preparation and delivery of the curriculum. Absorbing responsibility for budgetary work involves a larger concept of professional duty and relies upon a change of culture in the school. The benefits of good budgeting – apart from the legal requirement – can be shown to have substantial benefits for everyone in the organization and management of their school.

In the process of budget preparation, negotiation and follow-up, objectives have to be enumerated, clarified and put in priority order. The budget helps to bring into focus the critical actions which have to be taken and provides a comprehensive picture of the entire organization and its state of development. It is possible to adjudicate between various developments which may impede each other and keep an order of priority for a range of projects under review. This may have the advantage of mitigating conflict between individuals, groups, or departments which could otherwise have a damaging effect on morale and be financially wasteful. The subsequent controlling of operations according to the budget provides early warning of problems. In retrospect, the budget provides a basis for individual, group or departmental performance and may thereby be a positive motivator towards *better* professional performance.

The budget as a measure of staff performance, however, is above all a measure of senior management performance. It can be the means of cultivating good practice. To this end a five-point check list can be used in association with budget preparation, negotiation and control as follows.

1. Having established budget routines with dates which permit punctuality, and give adequate notice and room for dealing with unexpected difficulties.
2. Having good documentation which provides accurate and up-to-date management accounts, together with inventories which are complete.
3. Infusing a sense of urgency in business dealings, particularly over the budget, and ensuring that the budget reflects the views and interests of a wide range of persons.
4. Identifying external developments and their full significance for the school in advance so that preparations can be made to solve specific problems to which they give rise.
5. Taking remedial action promptly to correct performance failure and variance from budget, and producing prompt and accurate reports and accounts.

As the nomenclature of financial management becomes more familiar to everyone in schools, certain important concepts will become more clearly understood. For example, there are some fundamental distinctions to be made. The concept of 'cash' covers the visible activity of making payments and obtaining receipts. With a starting figure at the beginning of an accounting period – say, the school year – an individual, group or department records all payments made out of that figure and at the end of the period is able to strike a balance by taking into account anything left unspent, care being taken to retain all source documents such as orders and receipts.

The concept of 'accruals' is required where a large number of transactions is involved, some of which are spread over more than one accounting period. Items in annual accounts might not necessarily be received or paid for by the end of the financial year. For example, licence fees for television or motor vehicles may spread over the second half of one accounting period and the first half of the next. The accruals basis is to show costs incurred as expenses in the accounting year when the revenue to which they relate is acknowledged. On this basis the Profit and Loss Account – usually known as the Revenue Account – is meant to match income and expenditure in terms of overall and inclusive *value* rather than in terms of cash transactions and as such is a measure of the operating performance of the school over the given period. The Balance Sheet is a statement of what is owned and what is owed at the particular time in question – such as the final day of the school year. These assets and liabilities are shown as cash equivalents. Non-monetary assets such as land, vehicles, buildings, stock and materials may be shown at *acquisition* cost or may be written off altogether at the point of acquisition.

The second main distinction to be made is between 'capital' and 'revenue expenditure'. Capital is definable as expenditure on items which in turn increase the revenue-generating capacity of the organization in due course. An obvious example of this is the building of a new block or the refurbishment of existing science laboratories which could facilitate a larger intake of pupils and make it more attractive for pupils to enrol. But it refers also to such items as the purchase of a new photocopier. In contrast, revenue expenditure enables the operation to continue at existing levels. This would apply to the repair of existing assets – such as broken windows, science equipment or the photocopier. Capital costs are conceived as fixed costs and are shown as fixed assets in a Balance Sheet, whereas revenue expenditure involves variable costs shown as expenses in the Profit and Loss Account.

The third necessary and important distinction is to be made between 'assets' and 'liabilities'. A fixed asset is that which is purchased and retained to carry on the work of the school. A current asset is that which is purchased for resale or for processing (adding value) and converting into cash, or cash itself. Liabilities are current if due within the accounting period, or long term if due after the current accounting period has ended.

The final distinction can be made between profit- and non-profit-making organizations. The former must build up profits to survive by meeting increased costs, inflation, and the need to re-invest and where necessary to expand. Schools are primarily non-profit-making organizations though numerous ways of supplementing official grant income are employed. Nevertheless, it is equally important in schools to get value for money in the use of grant income and in this pursuit there are opportunities for making a surplus which may be construed as a profit.

The financial management of a school is subject to public audit. The job of a public auditor is to see that the money which is supplied from public sources is properly spent and accounted for. This includes ensuring that books, records and internal controls have been established and kept in proper working order and that the accounting system overall is right for the school and takes care of all transactions, which are then presented in an accurate and intelligible form. The accounts are compared with other records to establish that stated assets and liabilities actually exist and are fairly valued and stated, as are resulting profits or losses. The auditor also has to confirm that legal and accounting standards have been met. With the passage of a few years, many opportunities for using comparative data can arise from the accounting records. A record of expenditure for particular items, for example on scientific equipment, can be used for publicity purposes and the recruitment of staff and pupils. Per capita expenditure matched against achievements under the National Curriculum or external examinations – showing low-cost production, for example – might be valuable for the same purpose.

Evidence of prudent financial management and the generation of surpluses might be good for encouraging subscriptions from public bodies, grants from industry or gifts from benefactors. Showing profits or surpluses in relation to the capital employed or the official grant under formula funding is known as *ratio analysis*. It would include the record of previous years and could be compared with that for schools of similar size and composition or, more aggressively, with a school's direct competitors if needs be as an exercise in comparative unit costs.

A useful document produced annually could be 'A Statement of Sources and Application of Funds'. This would explain where funds have originated and how they have been used in simple terms for general consumption. It would also show how the financial position has changed since the previous issue but hopefully that liquidity prevails in there being a surplus of current assets over current liabilities. Funds in this case would mean working capital which for the school includes cash, stocks, inventories and debtors. An increase in working capital means either an increase in one or more of these, or a decrease in creditors. Similarly a decrease in working capital means either a decrease in one or more of these or an increase in creditors.

On the material – as opposed to the human – side of management the critical function is to manage the budget strictly to reach defined objectives applied both to the current annual budget in place and the longer-term budget details proposed

---

Effective financial control

The survival of the organization and the realization of its objectives as contained in the School Plan depends upon effective financial control. The School Plan is a statement compiled at any chosen point in time to show the school's asset values and financial balances, together with its agreed and costed objectives – including those already being implemented and those that have been newly formulated. Thereafter, periodic tests of progress may be made as steps on the way to the development of a modified School Plan. Such interim reviews are for comparing actual performance with what was intended so that corrective action can be taken as necessary. A School Plan needs to cover a reasonable period of time, relating to the obvious cycles of activity which are natural to the school, such as the school year and the length of time a pupil normally expects to stay in the school. It should be sufficient to provide for short-term, medium-term and long-term objectives. The School Plan is the pivot for the entire financial management of the school. Looked at as a *process*, this financial management includes five functions, which can be modelled as follows.

Function 1 Assessing the current position
- collecting facts and figures, including staff and consumer complaints
- taking into account HMI and LEA reports, rules and requirements
- applying internal and external performance indicators
- requiring self-monitoring by individuals and groups on how they are meeting their declared objectives
- reviewing the external standing of the school, market forces and recruitment prospects for pupils, staff and governors

Function 2 Determining the desired position
- identifying overlooked obligations
- grasping new opportunities which have appeared
- eliminating uneconomic activities, disaffection and underperformance
- finding economies of scale which are feasible
- undertaking new investment

Function 3 Deciding the action needed to reach the desired position from the current position
- reallocating the same funds
- generating additional funds
- restructuring and retraining the staff
- regrouping the pupils
- modifying the curricular programme

Function 4 Taking the action needed
- holding meetings and making plans and preparations
- allocating responsibilities with dates
- setting objectives in priority order with deadlines
- reviewing progress
- solving problems and correcting variances

Function 5 Monitoring and evaluating the newly achieved position
- reviewing objectives
- testing performances of individuals and groups
- checking expenditure
- obtaining feed-back from those affected by the changes
- comparing facts and figures with those of the previous position

Objectives feature at the centre of financial management. They have to be generated, refined, clarified and given priority order at all levels. They need to have costs attached to them and they need to have time tags attached to them. That objectives are set at all and by whatever means is a vital responsibility of management at any level. How they are actually set is perhaps a key factor separating effective managers from the ineffective.

Since it is obviously important that everyone who is to contribute to the realization of an objective should know what that objective actually is, it must follow that objectives need to be circulated, publicized and reiterated as often as necessary. But it is not so obvious that the best way of achieving this is to ensure that the formulation of objectives is by a process which actively involves all those who are going to be responsible for their realization in practice at the particular level concerned. The task is to engage the hearts and minds fully in the drive to reach the objective.

With reference to Chapter 2, it can be therefore somewhat academic to argue specifically for either a 'top down' strategy or a 'bottom up' strategy with respect to the managerial style used to secure the setting of objectives. The top down strategy means that one person or few decide what is to be done on the basis of either adequate or inadequate information, fact, whim or intuition. These decisions are communicated as objectives for the many, suitably translated for application at various levels throughout the organization, accompanied perhaps by explanations and subject to later clarification and modification. The bottom up strategy means that individuals or suitably defined sub-groups are asked to prepare their own future work in terms of a set of objectives which maintains or modifies by deletion or addition their existing activities and job content. Priorities, deadlines and costings need to be attached. Top management then has the job of collating and analysing such offerings in the light of school-wide considerations such as public standing, recruitment levels, legal shortcomings, academic strengths and weaknesses, and parental opinion. But essentially it is a matter of adjudicating the wide variety of objectives which signal what organization members themselves want to do. Neither strategy is pure in practice. In any case, some people like to work in a more directive organizational climate, others in a more volitional one. The essential need is for the working individual to be completely familiar with an objective because he or she identifies with it for one reason or another – be it a strong desire to please a caring boss or because there is an opportunity for considerable autonomy.

Both negotiation and reconciliation inevitably feature in the process of applying either a top down or a bottom up strategy, since objectives are usually too numerous, too mutually contradictory, and too costly for a given budget. In the end, the critical dialogue is between objectives and resources. Finances determine the School Plan.

The first claim on the budget is that of unavoidable costs. This is a somewhat subjective concept since at least at the margin what one school may regard as unavoidable another may not. A reserve fund may be allocated, leaving the rest of the budget available for variable distribution. Such a reserve fund may be allocated for contingencies such as unexpected price rises or supply cover – although the latter can be made subject to separate insurance cover. This reserve or contingency fund should not be trimmed down in response to strong bids from various quarters in the organization which have a lot of influence. It can always be brought into use later in the financial year for general distribution when it becomes clear that it is not needed for its original purpose. It is prudent always to assume nil or certainly a very conservative level of windfall income, such as that arising from sales or from parent–teacher social activities.

Under local financial management every element of school life needs to be costed out and a level and kind of use or activity identified for each. Every member of the teaching and non-teaching staff needs to think in cost terms with respect to both animate and inanimate elements. When the budget is up and running every individual should know

- his or her operational objectives
- the cost limits attached to them
- that he or she is accountable for financial performance in the job substantially based on these terms
- that eventual staff appraisal will take account of that performance

The assumption made is that every individual at his or her own particular level of responsibility in the organization has helped to draw up the School Plan and is able to control costs for that designated area of responsibility.

For the successful control of the budget a number of other mechanisms need to be in place. Any standing orders laid down by the local education authority must be observed. Beyond those, the governors and head may devise a set of rules and procedures of their own to suit local circumstances. For instance, they might establish dates at which automatic reviews of expenditure take place. Important rules would certainly include the prohibition of the same person placing an order and also making the payment for it. Others might include clear statements of the range of discretion of individuals and sub-groups, for example, the maximum size of expenditure for a single item, virement within a derivative budget and tradeoffs between two derivative budget holders before getting authorization from a superordinate.

The management responsibility is to see that enough rules and procedures are adopted to prevent fraud, anticipate overspending and have a continuing and accurate knowledge of the overall financial position but not more than the minimum needed to meet these objectives whilst avoiding the imposition of unnecessary work. When the master budget is reviewed part of that review would be to require the holders of sub-budgets to supply the following information:

- actual expenditure to date
- profiled expenditure i.e. what should have been spent by that date
- projected expenditure to the end of the financial year
- variances from the original plan
- committed expenditure, i.e. orders placed but not yet paid for

Corrective action by the budget holders themselves needs to be taken as soon as variances become known and supposing that the variance is not due simply to the payment of bills ahead of schedule. At school level strategic corrective action may be necessary when all the sub-budgets are analysed. For example, in an unusually bad winter there may have been widespread overspending on heating and lighting, needing an immediate conservation of energy order or the making of savings elsewhere.

Staffing costs are proportionately so large a part of the budget that a constant watch on how they are spent needs to be kept. The overall numbers of staff and the grades of those staff are the chief variables but other considerations can lead to economies. Job content analysis, for example, may show that administrative work undertaken by teachers might be concentrated sufficiently for the employment of a non-teaching member of staff, the costs for whom can be covered by a rationalization of the work content of the teachers. Costs may be shared between two or more schools for both teaching and non-teaching staff on the hiring side and in respect of retraining.

Space is an important cost factor. It is easy to incur unnecessary premises costs. This may be obvious with regard to wasteful heating and lighting but less obvious when a school suffers from congested and insufficient office space and at the same time has an empty classroom. A constant review of the use of total space available is advisable since the inefficient use of space can lead to the expensive use of staffing. The concept of optimum mix of space, staffing and pupil grouping needs to be centre stage at operational level to achieve financial efficiency. The allocation of these resources must reflect the school's objectives but the objectives in the first place need to have been costed so that the cost of various mixes make it possible to determine which objectives can be pursued.

Space can also provide additional earnings. Whilst the main strategy must be to make the most efficient use of grant income, a school can also supplement this by commercial initiatives of its own. The smaller the school the greater the proportion of its total income this can be. There are well-established possible ways of doing this but enterprising schools are constantly seeking new ways of generating additional income. A junior school obtained bankrupt stock and made £500 in a month for the purchase of computers. A secondary school hired out its bursar to neighbouring schools to provide them with some financial management assistance. But space is a potentially lucrative source of regular income. Routine letting should of course cover all costs, including the caretaker's overtime, energy, and the cost of any time incurred by professional staff who are taken away from educational duties. School premises are variously able to generate such income but only when they are strictly surplus to educational requirements. This mostly relates to the time of day, yet not necessarily so. A school which reserves a considerable area for parental parking needs to show that (a) this is good for the image of the school and serves publicity purposes, (b) that off-site parking is not a readily accessible alternative, and (c) that safety factors are taken into account both for the users and the school population on site. But above all it needs to show what the return on asset value is for the school. It could be held to pay for itself by way of enhanced parental and public esteem leading to better recruitment. It could be made subject to parking fees or be directly used for educational purposes.

Marketing skills

Marketing has become the inclusive concept for all that is needed to safeguard the well-being and survival of the organization by external means. It embraces activities which improve the wider public image of the organization, its standing as a neighbour in the local community, its reputation as an employer and as a place in which to work, and, above all, the demand levels for its goods or services and the esteem in which they are held, affected as they are by the organization's capacity for self-projection and its ability to persuade others to purchase or use its products. It is a very substantial part of the total management task. If total management is conceived as a sphere, production itself forms one hemisphere and marketing depicted in this way forms the other.

During the final quarter of the twentieth century, economic activity has been marked by significant and widespread deregulation both within the frontiers of sovereign national states and between them. Private-sector organizations have been primarily affected but those in the public sector too have been included in a vast movement to increase the discretionary powers of organizations of all kinds. Schools have been caught up in this movement and no longer have the sheltered existence once taken for granted. Such greater autonomy at once exposes the school to greater risks of managerial error and less than optimal survival. Hence there is a need for schools to consider the external dimension of their existence as never before. A part of the teacher's portfolio of professional skills needs to be devoted to marketing.

The concept of marketing the school to many may seem irrelevant. Children and young people are obliged to attend school by law. Many parents as well as their offspring regard school attendance as an alien sub-cultural experience to be avoided if possible. Yet there is so much scope for persuading dissident and indifferent groups of the benefits of schooling and wherever families have a choice of schools there is heightened advantage in marketing for the sake of recruitment figures.

For a marketing policy to work successfully there may need to be a fundamental shift in staff attitudes. With a previously captive market, attitudes could afford to be passive whereas open-market conditions require active attitudes and positive conduct. It is a matter of becoming consumer conscious. Many ingredients form the mix for good marketing but among the most important ones for the teacher to secure are the following.

1. Supplying full and accurate information promptly at various levels to increase knowledge of the school in the market.
2. Developing personal contacts, joining other organizations and being involved in community affairs to create a network of influence and channels of communication.
3. Taking pride in pleasing those who form the current or potential market to the extent of having a businesslike attitude and conducting matters in a businesslike way, and being able wherever possible to accommodate individual preferences and requests against standard arrangements and procedures.
4. Taking complaints seriously, turning them into consumer satisfaction and auditing them over a period of time with a view to achieving zero defects and zero defections.
5. Making the most of the school's specific and unique competences and features as well as its routine achievements by written and verbal means.

Marketing the school requires its own strategy and it needs to be adaptive to meet ever-changing conditions. Perceptions and demands in the market itself change and the products – what can be offered by the school – vary as the leadership, staff and pupil population in the school change over a period of time. Successful marketing is likely to depend upon the internal realization of four stages of development. These four appear overall in sequence but may be seen to overlap insofar as all sections of the school do not complete their contributions to each stage simultaneously.

The first stage is efficiency. This means paying one's way, remaining liquid, guarding the cash flow, reducing waste and generally matching income and expenditure with the best possible results. The achievement of this stage can be easily documented and made known.

The second stage is quality. This means fine tuning production. Vague and unrealistic achievements are not entertained. Specific and critical improvements are targeted. Quality increases in any dimension of school work and activity of 5 per cent per annum amount to substantial success. Quality depends upon staff attitudes and effort but also on what can be induced in the pupil directly and indirectly through the parent. It can be made known through homework or taking completed work home, through the annual targets and occasional examinations of the National Curriculum, public examination results, sporting and cultural events, and by formal written reports for individual pupils and for the school as a whole.

The third stage is flexibility. The first two stages of efficiency and quality presuppose simplicity of structure and product but as time passes attempts need to be made to meet finer variations in demand and individual satisfactions, affecting staff, pupils and parents. The school becomes less standard and more complex as it adapts to changing conditions. The point is that efficiency and quality have to be maintained whilst this happens. Sometimes they are lost in the transition, requiring a reversal until they can be recovered.

The fourth stage is innovation. On the basis of the strength of technology or know-how resulting from the successful completion of the first three stages, the school is able to plan and implement its own deliberate innovation which could have important effects on its reputation and its ability to recruit staff and pupils. Such innovation may be in its structure, curriculum or external activities, any of which may be intended to meet a newly emerging need or indeed to generate new interest and demand in the market.

Looking at marketing from this point of view is significant because it carries home the need for the school to be market-led in dealing with its internal management. It also provides an order of priorities for busy teachers who are often weighed down with the cares and responsibilities of the immediate day's work. It can be especially helpful for those who take over a new responsibility or post and are in need of a strategy for action in talking with colleagues or the staff and governors as a whole.

Local financial management can give a new perspective and perhaps a new impetus to marketing. Marketing the school can be costly but the outlay can be cost effective. The school needs to attract pupils in an age of parental choice so it needs to present itself favourably and as a school which meets the aspirations of the community it serves. This may be handled by some market research on parental opinion and expectations but also by ensuring that the visible aspects of the school are reassuring –

freedom from litter, a polite and helpful secretary to answer the telephone and receive visitors, a welcoming entrance with good signposting and display work to catch the eye of the visitor.

Promotional material can be the subject of internal design and production aimed at increasing recruitment and resources. Access to the media can have the same purpose. Complaints, frequently regarded as irksome, can almost become accounting items in the sense that they can be systematically collected, reported and recorded. Corrective action where possible can be taken at once, but otherwise complaints can be fed into the information system and find their way ultimately into having effects on objectives and the budget. The volume of complaints can become an index of school performance.

All in all then the school is a workplace which demands a very substantial range of skills, augmented by those which arise from having financial autonomy. The school may be said therefore to have its own technology. Organizational technology has been defined as the characteristic way in which an organization goes about its work to achieve the output it wants. This concept applies to the school as much as it does to every other kind of organization. The school resembles other kinds of educational organizations in many respects and non-educational organizations in some respects. It retains, however, a number of unique features.

Owing to the complex nature of the school as an organization, an adequate conceptual approach is needed for purposes of control. Uncertainty over cause and effect in educational activity is a dominant factor affecting technology, and must be taken into account when devising strategies for solving organizational problems in schools. Recognizable practices that are characteristic of schools may nevertheless be identified and analysed, including the collective and personal skills of the teaching staff.

Control in organizations is achieved and sustained by facing up to the endless succession of problems which arise. These range from the trivial to the complex. Schools should have their own strategies and methods for solving problems, including their own *ad hoc* research capability.

4 *Shaping the organization*

The word structure is used in many disciplines, including biology, economics, mathematics, physics and sociology. In building and engineering fields, the concept is applied to an arrangement of materials which can bear loads in excess of its own weight. The familiar sight of steel frameworks on construction sites and bridges made of stone, timber or steel are obvious.

Similarly, when used in organizations, the concept of structure refers to an arrangement of human relationships. Given that the body of people in question – such as the teaching staff of a school – has a definable, collective task, the structure enables them to accomplish it. Structure therefore, is an instrumental device and not an end in itself. It helps the teaching staff of a school to achieve more than would otherwise be achieved as a sum of the independent, uncoordinated efforts of the individuals concerned. Structure is an enabling mechanism.

> Structure is the deliberate patterning of relationships between organization members

The elements of structure

Structure as an enabling mechanism applies to all groups as organizations. The crew of a jumbo-jet want to achieve a safe and successful flight. The staff of a school want to achieve the acceptable education of its pupils. In all such cases, the current and emerging work of the organization can at any time be analysed and apportioned to the individuals who share collective responsibility for it. The portion of the total work of the organization which comes to the individual is that individual's *job*, and constitutes his or her contribution to the organization. This is irrespective of whether or not the individual plays any part in deciding what his or her own job shall be.

The teacher's job consists of both instructional duties – working with pupils – and organizational duties – working with colleagues and other adults inside and outside the school. In both cases teachers may be subject to detailed direction over what they do and how they must do it, or they may be accorded maximum freedom of decision over both. These are theoretical extremes between which reality variously lies. In the first case – diminished direction – the job is defined by a superordinate teacher. In the latter case – maximum discretion – the assumption is made that the teacher is able to make the necessary judgements and selection of behaviour himself. In both cases the *job* of the teacher is the individual's contribution to the organizational total but the *way* in which he or she may discharge the job differs.

In attempting to discharge the job an individual expects to be able to exercise some influence on the actions of others. The justification for this expectation is that each person, as an acknowledged member of the organization, has an agreed job to do in the interests of the whole. Every individual in respect of a particular job, therefore, may be said to have the right to expect other members of the organization to take due notice of the fact that an agreed contribution must be discharged. On a logical basis, this right should be appropriate to the job, and this is the *authority* which an individual who undertakes the job expects to possess as a result.

Among organization members, the willingness and ability to accept and handle the authority that belongs to their respective jobs vary. Some members feel inhibited as a result of their own personality make-up, the intimidation of others, lack of training, or perhaps uncertainty. People who are new to a post experience such uncertainty. As a head has recorded: 'I had the sensation of being a stranger entering a family gathering. After two weeks this feeling has largely disappeared and I am beginning to feel part of the organization rather than a decoration on top of the cake. The latter impression was caused because I was uncertain.' (quoted by Dunham 1979).

Uncertainty may also arise from lack of support. The following verbatim quotation came from a team leader in a middle school.

> Only very recently has the headmaster put his full self into the running of the school. Until this academic year, each team leader was left to manage things as he or she would with no support at all from the top. Only if something backfired or if outside agencies were called in did the head notice the existence of his team leaders who were virtually running the school. This was not a happy situation. Things are now improving and joint decisions are made, but the memory of what went before still colours one's vision.

In contrast, some individuals are greedy for authority and will increase their own authority by various means at the expense of others. Difficult and sometimes bizarre situations can arise from such unchecked movements in the distribution of authority which is inconsistent with their responsibilities. It may also happen between teaching and non-teaching staff. A school secretary or caretaker has been known to exercise authority which reached well beyond the particular duties for which he or she was responsible, affecting decisions which influenced the educational provisions which teachers desired for the pupils.

The under- or over-exercise of authority relative to the job in classical thinking about organization has serious implications. Those who, for any reason, do not exercise the authority which their jobs require are holding back the development of the organization and reducing its efficiency and effectiveness. Means should be found to remove any obstacles to the exercise of the authority required, or to supply any assistance needed to redress the situation so that such individuals are able to discharge their jobs properly.

One of these obstacles, of course, may be that others are exerting an overbearing influence and have assumed too much authority themselves. A typical case of this occurs in schools when the head of the school decentralizes decision making in designated areas to team leaders who themselves do not adopt the same policy in respect of their members, or do so differentially across the different teams, groups or departments.

It is a responsibility of management to be vigilant over such matters and to take appropriate action. If the under- or over-exercise of authority is characteristic among senior teachers, the head of the school must work to redress the situation. If it occurs among members of a sub-group, such as a year team in a junior school or a department in a secondary school, the team leader or head of department would need to take the necessary action. This is simply to elaborate the assertion that 'structuring' is an important responsibility in the management function.

In the event that a job and the authority attaching to it are projected for a period of time as constant, the individual concerned assumes, or is accorded, a *position* in the organization. A position, therefore, enshrines the expectation that a person's job is conceived in a generalized form which stresses continuity, repetition and regularity. Positions point to functions. It might be the function of a particular position in a large school – the deputy-head, for example – to deal with day-to-day crises. This he does on a basis of continuity, repetition and regularity.

The critical ingredients of structure are
- job
- authority
- position

Job, authority and position are the elements of structure, as illustrated in Figure 4.1. When the question is asked 'What is the structure of a school?', information is being sought by the questioner which will lead him to an understanding of the distribution of jobs, authority and positions within it. The possession of such information makes the comparison of different schools possible.

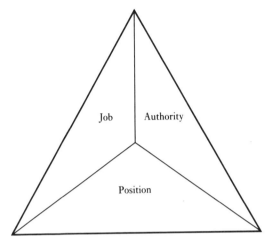

Figure 4.1 The elements of structure

The use of titles or designations

The job, authority and position of each organization member are inevitably conveyed by a title or designation, which seldom, if ever, conveys all that is entailed in behavioural terms for an individual member. This is particularly true of 'people organizations' like schools.

It is a relatively straightforward matter to designate a teacher in a primary school to show that the teacher's preoccupation is expected to be the knowledge, abilities and concern pertinent to the process of learning to read and developing reading. The job is clear – teaching children to read and improving their reading skills. The teacher's authority will derive from the demonstrable skills and knowledge possessed and their effectiveness in terms of pupil performance levels. Other teachers will be quick to take note, unless they are perverse in attitude. The actual *position* of the teacher in the structure, however, may involve more than that conveyed by this particular phrase. The designation may not specify 'curriculum leader *and general teacher*' even though these words represent a full and more accurate title.

Similarly, a teacher designated 'year leader' in a junior school has the job of leading a team. Leadership qualities as well as teaching capacity will form the basis of the teacher's authority. The position of 'year leader' implies that there are also team members and other year leaders.

In a secondary school, to be a 'geography teacher' signifies the job of teaching one particular subject rather than any other subject and implies the need to be competent to do whatever is necessary in the school to teach geography well. Again, knowledge and skill pertaining to that subject and its pedagogy will form the basis of the authority needed. The teacher's position is that of a 'class member' rather than 'head of geography' or 'deputy-head'.

Even these examples of titles or designations, however, are quite inadequate indices of all the knowledge and behavioural skills which any teacher needs to exercise to be an effective organization member. It becomes more difficult still when one tries to infer what titles such as 'curriculum coordinator', 'head of department', 'deputy-head', or 'head' represent in a particular structure at a particular time.

At the stage of planning a structure, whether for a school as a whole or any part of it, the plan is 'ideal' in the sense that it represents a rational and logically articulated view of what is needed to make an effective organization. In practice, however, actual people – with all the variability of reality that is implied by the phrase – must give life to the planned structure and transform the drawing-board intentions and hopes into operational structure. A vital task of management is continually to match real people to the structure that an organization requires to discharge its task. In the case of the school this task is the adaptive education of young people.

Titles or designations then are inclusive terms for jobs, authority and positions. They provide a shorthand for depicting structure. They are subject to varying interpretations, according to the knowledge, understanding and expectations of the incumbent, the influence and expectations of colleagues and the intentions of those who offered the post in the first place. All of these considerations would be expected to form the content of 'job specifications' and 'job descriptions' which if written, can quickly become out of date and need to be constantly revised, probably by the job holders themselves.

The political aspect of structure

With a high staff turnover, structural changes may be readily made. Staff who remain can be offered jobs, authority and positions vacated by those who have left. Alternatively, structure may be thought out afresh so that remaining staff are offered new jobs, authority and positions, leaving the residual vacancies to be filled by newcomers.

Structural changes are nearly always exhilarating for some and threatening for others. The risks involved, therefore, must be calculated. In times of stable staffing or low staff turnover, it is very tempting to allow structure to become static. It takes time, effort and, perhaps, stress and strain to achieve smooth working relations – to establish an effective operational structure – as a teaching staff. If the number of pupils in a school is changing, it is likely that restructuring will be unavoidable.

Minimal structural change may well suit the teaching staff of a school. The critical determinant of structural change, however, should be the changing nature of the perceived organizational task. It is unlikely that the pattern of knowledge, expertise and experience represented by a particular structure will for long avoid a mismatch with the more volatile interests and needs of successive entries of pupils in a world where inexorable change is the dominant reality.

It is not that structure *ought* to be subject to constant modification *per se*, but that structure is the vehicle for getting the work of organizations done, and is essentially temporary or *ad hoc* in nature. Unfortunately, however, the constant change of structure is almost certain to generate frustration, anger and perhaps unhappiness, and even breakdown, in some members. Teachers are no exception to the rule that nobody likes excessive uncertainty and discontinuity. Furthermore, changes in structure may increase the career potential of some staff and decrease that of others.

Everyone likes time to master a job and to feel that he or she is making a real and visible contribution to the organization. Structural changes, therefore, imply the exercise of political art, involving delicate and painstaking work on the part of those whose responsibility it is to initiate them. The successful negotiation and implementation of such changes are at the heart of good management. As a human process, changing the structure requires sensitivity and concern. As a political process it requires persuasiveness and firmness. Both require the ability to grasp the critical factors and the skills to articulate them. In short, consideration and initiation go together.

With the passing of time, structural changes are made to meet new demands or to cope more effectively with old ones. Often these are accomplished on an *ad hoc* basis, a review of the structure as a whole being avoided for internal political reasons. By custom and usage everyone knows the job, authority and position of everyone else. Adjustments are soon learnt and assimilated. This process is usually adequate in small schools but the larger the school the more likely it is that formal definitions and greater precision will be necessary. The object after all is to have a firm structure which means that each person has a clear place and brief within it and that this is known to and understood by others. A lack of firm structure is not uncommon, arising more from operational changes with the passing of time than as a result of original design at a starting point or interim major revision.

A reasonable degree of definition and precision applies equally to senior and junior staff. There is often confusion in the mind of a junior member of non-teaching or teaching staff, for example, over the exact responsibilities of each of a number of deputy heads who may be variously seeking to maximize their personal standing and chances of promotion.

It is argued by some that in humanistic organizations like schools – perhaps with the implication that organizations other than schools and the like are not or cannot be humanistic – definition and precision should have only a minimal place in the structure. The resulting concept which has been called 'loose coupling' means that jobs, authority and position can be made to overlap to an extended degree if necessary. This still requires definitions of what is overlapped, however. It may imply various degrees of interchangeability of tasks or areas of responsibility. But this too is a form of structure and needs appropriate definition and description, notably as to what is interchanged, presented for the structure as a whole. Avoidance or postponement can so easily be rationalized.

Ideally, the structure of a school should closely reflect the current overall task which the school faces. In practice, however, the structure of any organization nearly always contains maladaptive features. These are jobs, authority and positions which once made good sense but no longer meet the needs of the organization in terms of new tasks being required of it. The constant change in the quantitative aspects of the school's task is inevitable. The reasons are plain: the increase in knowledge, staff and pupil turnover, the demands which parents and employers make of the curriculum, pedagogical factors and many other variables all combine to present any school with the need for continual adaptation.

Unusually, a teacher may join others to open a new school, and thus to structure its organization for the first time. Typically, a teacher joins an on-going school and will be required to fit into a predetermined structure. If the structuring has been skilfully accomplished, the school stands the best chance of experiencing smooth operating conditions. If the structuring has been careless, then operating conditions are likely to be difficult.

People are sometimes understandably reluctant to change successful and well-established structures. This applies particularly to schools where the staff turnover is at a low rate. This follows since, by definition, the overall, complex pattern of interpersonal relations implied by the concept of structure has been established, learned and accepted as a *modus vivendi*, with few newcomers to upset it.

Should an old structure prove inadequate in practice, a modification of it will emerge, based on the unanticipated realities of the personal capacities of the people concerned. In such a case, individuals lose either jobs, authority and positions as new pressures on the organization and new members within it make their presence felt.

Of the three elements, job, authority and position, the last is the one which occasions most difficulty in designing and modifying the structure of a school. Positions are signalled by the appellation of titles and attract

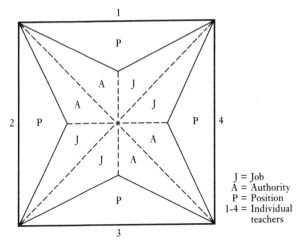

Figure 4.2 Structural stability and adaptation

J = Job
A = Authority
P = Position
1-4 = Individual
teachers

differential monetary rewards. Positions, rather than jobs or authority, are least subject to change. Positions, in addition, are a powerful determinant of the expectations of the incumbents and those around them with regard to the personal capacities of position-holders. The idea of positions gives stability to the structure. It may also infuse rigidity into the structure, in that positions are more permanent and reflect the people in them. Rigid structures are, by definition, maladaptive to necessary changes in the curriculum and organization of the school. The practice of making positions permanent, therefore, results in diminished structural adaptability. An individual may remain in command (position) of something (job) but not in control (authority) of it.

Figure 4.2 illustrates the fact that position, having relative permanence, gives stability to structure, whilst jobs and authority may be relatively flexible and subject to dispute. The diagram represents organizational structure in the case of four people. Each has a formal position, P, which basically distinguishes them as organization members. Their respective jobs and authority, however, are subject to relatively easy change or redistribution, given the total task which they must collectively discharge. This is represented in the central area of the diagram with dotted boundary lines. It illustrates what is implied by the practice known as 'job rotation'.

Depicting structure – traditional forms

Attempts to depict the organizational structure of the school as a whole traditionally takes the form of pyramidal shapes, either flat or tall, as in

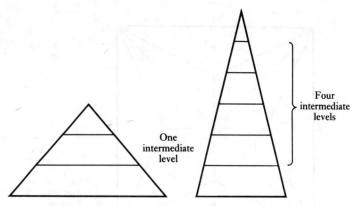

Figure 4.3 Flat and tall pyramidal forms

Figure 4.3. A flat pyramid implies a less finely determined distribution of jobs (i.e. less specialization), few levels of authority and more individuals occupying similar positions as compared with a tall pyramid. In contrast, the tall pyramid represents a more finely determined distribution of jobs, many levels of authority and fewer individuals occupying similar positions. The former is said to have a short, and the latter a long, chain-of-command.

Examples of the flat pyramid are common in schools, especially in the primary sector. A junior school, for instance, might be depicted as in Figure 4.4. In this case, it is implied that each of the eight class teachers formally possess equal authority attaching to equal jobs and the same structural position. In reality, however, fine distinctions are probably made between the jobs, producing differential authority, even though positions in the structure remain formally equal. In practice, of the eight class teachers, several would receive additional salary allowances, known as incentive

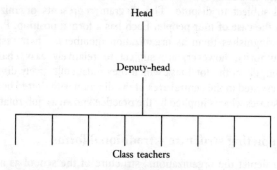

Figure 4.4 Flat pyramid in a junior school

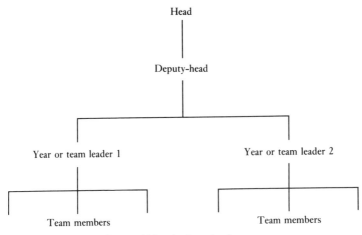

Figure 4.5 Tall pyramid in a junior school

allowances for undertaking special responsibilities. The money available for this might be devoted to larger payments to few staff or smaller payments to many staff. The former policy tends to create a taller pyramid, the latter a flatter pyramid.

In spite of the *formal* structure, as depicted, distinctions between teachers in practice create an informal structure. A likely basis for it in a junior school, for example, might be assumed differences of expertise required for teaching different age-groups. In a class-based school, teachers taking fourth-year pupils might assume – and others might ascribe to them – superior or superordinate positions compared with teachers taking a first-year group. This would be an example of *de facto* structure in contrast to the *de jure* structure as represented in the diagram. In *practice*, therefore, the school would have a tall pyramid, rather than the flat pyramid it claimed to have.

If the same school – whilst remaining exactly the same size, and with the same staff – decided to reorganize, a new structure would need to be determined. An example of a possible restructuring which it might adopt, implying a radical change, could be as in Figure 4.5. In structure, the organization has formally changed from being a flat pyramid to being a tall pyramid. There is now an additional intermediate management level, i.e. those who might be called team, group or year leaders. All three elements of structure – the distribution of job, authority and positions – have been subject to considerable revision.

Many questions affecting all ten teachers represented in Figure 4.5 remain to be answered. For example, what is the job of the deputy-head,

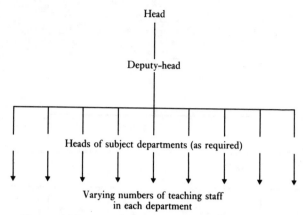

Figure 4.6 Flat pyramid in a secondary school

now that the two team leaders exist? Does the head delegate work to the deputy-head which he previously reserved for himself? If the head does this, what alternative work does he undertake? How does the position of the team members compare with the position the same people had when they were class teachers? Do they feel subject to more supervision or do they now have the opportunity for greater participation in the management of the school?

It is clear from this example that the pyramidal form is primarily concerned to show the command aspect of structural positions, and authority. In other words, the pyramid reveals the basic relations between people thought to be needed to give the organization a unitary direction. It shows one person as a position holder to whom another person in a subordinate position is formally answerable.

In large schools, particularly in the secondary sector, a flat pyramid would contain as many levels as the tall pyramid presented above for the junior school, as illustrated in Figure 4.6. If such a school decided to restructure, it could do so in one of two ways. First, it could decide to increase the number of positions as in Figure 4.7.

In this case a taller pyramid has been introduced by inserting the heads of faculty. This position represents a new centre of authority. Some rearrangement of jobs involving a number of people would have been necessary to create this additional position, with no change in the total number of personnel. It is likely that two of the former heads of department were promoted as heads of faculty and two former members of subject departments were promoted to replace the heads of department. Alternatively, the two new heads of faculty might be expected to retain their heads of subject positions. In both cases, the restructuring implies

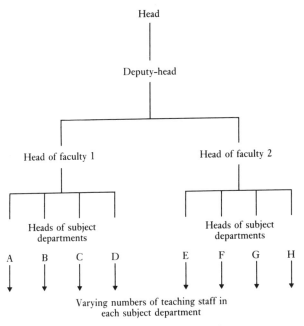

Figure 4.7 Tall pyramid in a secondary school

little disturbance in general and the job of each teacher remains essentially the same.

This is not so, however, if the school decided to restructure in the second way mentioned. In this case, a fundamental reconsideration of the job of every person in the old structure is involved. The particular outcome, as represented in Figure 4.8, results from deciding that the work of the school may be separated into pedagogical and administrative constituents.

A flat form of pyramid has been retained in this example, but there are really two such pyramids rather than one. Two structures formally co-exist. Each teacher reports to two superordinates. In the position of subject teacher, each teacher reports to a head of department. In the position of tutor-group leader, each teacher reports to a head of year. The basic separation of job content for everybody is reflected in the fact that two people now occupy the deputy-head's position.

Alternative bases.   A distinction may be drawn between the need for staff control and the need for operational efficiency. Figure 4.9 (page 112) assumes that two structures are simultaneously necessary to take account of this. A pyramidal form is required for handling certain factors

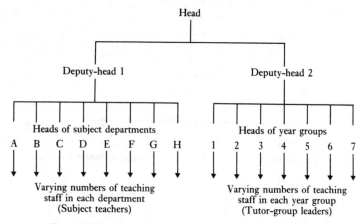

Figure 4.8 Dual pyramids in a secondary school

(e.g. hiring, firing, qualifications, performance review and promotion). This may be called the control structure. An *ad hoc* form is also required for handling the workflow on a programme-conceived basis.

Some actual structures from existing schools for teaching staff and governors are given as examples in the following tables.

Table 4.1 Teaching staff structure for a junior school of 235 pupils aged 7 to 11 with a head teacher and nine other teaching staff

Head
- Chief executive; chairing the management team; no timetable teaching but occasional relief teaching; responsible for the Parent–Teacher Association

Deputy head
- Member of management team on all matters of organizational development for the school as a whole
- Organization and development of the curriculum
- In-service education and training
- School grounds
- Educational visits
- Professional support to staff
- In charge of History, Geography and Religious Education in the National Curriculum

First teacher with 'B' incentive allowance
- Member of management team on all matters of organizational development for the school as a whole
- Organization and development of resources, resourced-based learning and library
- Festivals and celebrations throughout the school year
- Liaison with Infant Schools
- Assisting deputy head with educational visits

Table 4.1 (cont.)

- In charge of Special Needs in the National Curriculum
- In charge of English in the National Curriculum

Second teacher with 'B' incentive allowance
- Member of management team on all matters of organizational development for the school as a whole
- Pupil profiling system for the whole school
- Liaison with Secondary Schools and the local community
- Assisting deputy head with in-service education and training
- Assisting with photographic records, media liaison and publicity
- In charge of Science, and Design and Technology in the National Curriculum

Teacher with 'A' incentive allowance
- Assisting deputy head with day-to-day management
- Assisting with pupil profiling
- School Health and Safety Officer
- School sports and matches
- Assisting with Secondary School liaison
- Management of the staff room
- In charge of Music and Drama in the National Curriculum

First teacher with Main Scale salary
- Displays and exhibitions
- Assisting with Infant School liaison
- Assisting with Health and Safety
- Assisting with Parent–Teacher Association
- In charge of Art and Craft in the National Curriculum

Second teacher with Main Scale salary
- Support for newly qualified staff
- Care of student-teachers and visitors to the school
- Assisting with the organization and development of resources for the curriculum
- Staff rosters
- Assisting with festivals and celebrations
- In charge of Mathematics in the National Curriculum

Third teacher with Main Scale salary
- Assisting with staff-room management
- Assisting with Parent–Teacher Association
- Assisting with library
- Assisting with displays and exhibitions
- Assisting with the care of school grounds
- In charge of Health Education and Home Economincs in the National Curriculum

Fourth teacher with Main Scale salary
- Photographic records, media liaison and publicity
- Assisting with community liaison
- Assisting with school sports and matches
- In charge of Physical Education in the National Curriculum

Fifth teacher with Main Scale salary (part-time)
- Assisting with Special Needs in the National Curriculum

Table 4.2 Teaching staff structure for a secondary school of 760 students aged 13 to 18 with a head teacher and fifty-three other teaching staff

Those with management responsibilities are listed. All other members of the teaching staff are specialist subject teachers with a full teaching timetable

Head
- Chief executive; no timetable teaching
- Chairing the senior management team
- Manager for Year 11 students and Year 11 buildings
- In charge of Citizenship in the National Curriculum

First deputy head
- Overall coordination of the school's curriculum
- Manager of Curriculum Area 1 – English, Modern Languages and the Expressive Arts
- Assessment for Curriculum Area 1
- Staff appraisal for Curriculum Area 1
- Manager for Sixth-Form students and Sixth-Form buildings
- Manager of school sports centre
- In charge of Economics and Industrial Awareness in the National Curriculum

Second deputy head
- Overall responsibility for personnel management
- Staff development
- Manager of Curriculum Area 2 – Humanities and Physical Education
- Assessment for Curriculum Area 2
- Staff appraisal for Curriculum Area 2
- Assisting with overall coordination of the school's curriculum
- Liaison with industry and the community
- Manager of Year 9 students and Year 9 buildings
- In charge of Social and Personal Education in the National Curriculum

Senior teacher with 'E' incentive allowance
- Information technology throughout the school
- Manager of Curriculum Area 3 – Mathematics, Science and Technology
- Assessment for Curriculum Area 3
- Staff appraisal for Curriculum Area 3
- Manager for Year 10 students and Year 10 buildings
- In charge of Health Education and Environmental Education in the National Curriculum

Head of Mathematics with 'E' incentive allowance
- Professional tutor
- In charge of Mathematics in the National Curriculum

Head of Technology with 'E' incentive allowance
- In charge of Technology and Environmental Education in the National Curriculum

Head of Sixth Form with 'E' incentive allowance
- Records of achievement throughout the school
- Tutor for sixth-form students

These seven staff constitute the senior management team. The explicit policy attaching to their deployment is that it is designed to cope with the changes and

Table 4.2 (Cont.)

---

demands that will affect the school in the 1990s and that a system of job rotation will operate to give its members management development experience.

Teachers with 'D' incentive allowances

Head of Year 9
Head of Year 10
Head of Year 11
Head of Modern Languages
Head of English
Head of Humanities
Head of Expressive Arts
Head of Curriculum Support
Head of Science

Teachers with 'C' incentive allowances

Deputy to Head of Modern Languages
Head of Information Technology

Teachers with 'B' incentive allowances

Deputy to Head of Science
Deputy to Head of Mathematics
Deputy to Head of Technology
Deputy to Head of English
Deputy to Head of Humanities
Teacher in charge of Community Studies
Teacher in charge of Physical Education
Teacher in charge of Drama and Theatre Studies
Teacher in charge of Art
Teacher in charge of Careers Education
Coordinator for the Certificate of Proficiency in Vocational Education

Teachers with 'A' incentive allowances

Press Officer
Teacher in charge of Community Sports
Teacher in charge of Geography

A notable feature in both the junior and the secondary schools is the provision of an assistant or deputy who provides a formal understudy for important posts.

The secondary school concerned has a 30-period week. The two deputy heads have a 15-period remission for their extensive management duties. The other members of the Senior Management Team and the more senior of the incentive allowance postholders not in the Senior Management Team have remissions varying from three to ten periods per week according to seniority. Little or no remission time exists for those

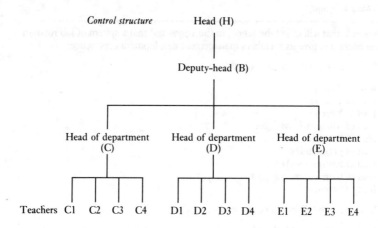

Operational structure

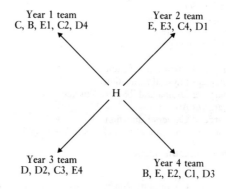

Figure 4.9 Control and operational forms of structure

teachers with considerable management responsibilities in the junior school.

The special feature of the structure in the secondary school is the fusion of academic and pastoral functions. The member of the Senior Management Team who is designated manager for a part of the entire curriculum (Curriculum Areas 1, 2 and 3) chairs meetings and coordinates all the duties at operational level which bear upon the individual student concerned. The job, authority and position of each of these three teachers as managers may be represented diagramatically as in Figure 4.10.

Now that school governors are in much larger numbers with wider

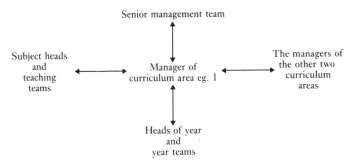

Figure 4.10 Structure for Merging Academic and Pastoral Interests

powers and real powers of policy and command, it is important to incorporate the governing body of a school formally within its structure. Tables 4.3 and 4.4 show examples of the structure of governing bodies. The initiative and guidance of the head to produce an effective structure within the governing body may be necessary in the absence of managerial acumen among the governors themselves.

Bearing in mind that structure involves job, authority and position, it is self-evident that the implications of choosing one structure rather than

Table 4.3 Structure within Primary School Governing Bodies

Example 1 Total 13 governors plus head: 261 pupils
  Sub-group for Health and Safety – 3 members plus head
  Sub-group for staffing – 5 members plus head
  Sub-group for buildings – 3 members plus head
  Sub-group for finance – 2 members plus head
There is no sub-group for the curriculum. Curriculum matters are dealt with on the basis of the Head's reports at full meetings of the governing body. The head and chairman of governors meet weekly. There are two meetings of the full governing body each term and at least two meetings of each sub-group each term. There is one meeting of parents each term which generates papers which go to the meeting of the governing body.

Example 2. Total 16 governors plus head: 345 pupils
  Sub-group for curriculum – 4 members plus head
  Sub-group for staffing – 4 members plus head
  Sub-group for buildings – 4 members plus head
  Sub-group for finance – 4 members plus head
There are two meetings of the full governing body each term. Sub-groups meet regularly twice per term but more often if required. There is a formal and systematic programme for governors to visit the school during the working day. Each governor has a watching brief for a particular part of the National Curriculum, including Special Needs so that the whole curriculum is covered.

Table 4.4 Structure within Secondary School Governing Bodies

Example 1 Total 14 governors plus one co-opted plus head: 760 students
  Sub-group for staffing – 3 members plus head
  Sub-group for staff appeals – 3 members
  Sub-group for finance – 6 members plus head
There are two meetings of the full governing body each term. Apart from the two appointed teacher governors, all six members of the senior management team attend every meeting of the full governing body with the head. They may speak but only the head may vote. Prior to each meeting of the full governing body the finance and staffing sub-groups meet. The former consists of the chair and vice-chairperson of the full governing body, the head, two parent governors and two teacher governors. The latter consists of three governors and the head. The two deputy heads attend each of these sub-group meetings. Financial and staffing business is taken at the full meetings of the governing body having been prepared by the sub-groups. All other business, including the curriculum is taken directly in full meetings of the governing body. Each governor monitors a particular part of curriculum so that the entire National Curriculum is covered. The governor concerned joins the interviewing panel for any staff appointments to the subject areas which he or she covers.

The three governors who deal with staff appeals regarding salaries, contracts and discipline are not members of any other sub-group. They meet as needed, calling in the head or others as they see fit. They are comprised of one parent governor, one local education authority governor and one Foundation governor, it being a church school.

Example 2 Total 14 governors (two of whom are also trustees) plus 3 further trustees plus head: 270 students
  Sub group for finance – 4 governors plus bursar plus head.
This is an independent school. There is one meeting of the full governing body per term. All matters are dealt with in full session except for financial business which is prepared by the special sub-group which meets prior to the main meeting. There are no teaching staff members of the governing body since staff are paid by the trust. Staff interests are looked after by one governor. There are two parent governors who directly represent parents and take care of their interests.

---

another, and then of changing the structure, are far-reaching. The implications for the work of the organization – the educational experience offered to the pupils – are potentially substantial. In addition, but related to the educational outcome, structure affects the morale, efficiency and effectiveness of the teachers themselves. Rapid or ill-handled changes in structure can have damaging repercussions.

These factors have become important matters of concern in various branches of research in organizational and managerial studies. Many studies have demonstrated that different structures reflect different value systems (Blau and Schoenher 1971). In the case of the school, different structures contain and reflect different assumptions about both pupils and teachers (Jennings 1975; Packwood 1977; Turner 1977). For example, it is possible at one extreme to be pessimistic about people at work, assuming that they need to be watched, directed and constantly stimulated as they seek to avoid effort and responsibility. In contrast, at the other extreme, it is possible to be optimistic about people at work, believing that the right conditions – particularly structure – will release creativity, effort and self-direction (McGregor 1960; 1967). In particular, as far as teachers are concerned, it is possible to assume either attenuated professionalism or extended professionalism (Hughes 1975).

An upsurge of studies in the field of organizational stress has also highlighted the differential outcomes from different structures (Wright 1975; Coleman 1976; Cooper and Marshall 1978; Melhuish 1978; Dunham 1990). The predicament of the individual within the structure has been a major theme of distinguished scholars for several decades (Argyris 1960). This work has been given new impetus by a focus on physiological, psychological and medical aspects of organizational structure. Within teaching, attention has been firmly drawn to the potential which the structure may have for damaging personal and professional life (National Association of Schoolmasters/Union of Women Teachers 1976).

In manufacturing and commercial organizations, the fact that stress may be caused by excessive noise or danger, for example, can be readily appreciated by everyone. It is less obvious that stress may result from the structural features and conditions which govern the organizational life of the individual.

In schools it has now been found, admitted and made plain that organizational stress is a risk factor in the occupational career of the teacher. Studies have emphasized the shortcomings of the school as a workplace (Dreeben 1973) and the intrinsic fatigue of teaching as an occupation (Pellegrin 1976). The most forceful and provocative illumination of this risk, however, has come from studies in Britain which attribute a great deal of stress to causes labelled as 'reorganization', 'role conflict' and 'role ambiguity' as well as poor working conditions. Teachers have administrative, pastoral and teaching work to do, but often suffer from uncertainty about the particular work they think they ought to be performing. Singular causation of stress is attributed to communication difficulties, barriers between teachers with different seniority and the kind of climate the head and senior staff generate (Thomas 1980).

When a teacher is caught in structural arrangements which are inimical to his welfare and development, extraordinary conduct may be produced by stress. Two examples may be given. In the first case, the head of newly amalgamated grammar and secondary modern schools appeared suddenly at the door of the crowded staff room at mid-morning break. He vigorously rang a miniature bell, bringing the noisy room to silence. He then harangued the staff about carelessness which might impair the school's reputation. A teacher had persistently accused a pupil of negligently losing a homework book. Finally, the parents had made representations in their son's defence. As a result, the Head had searched the classroom concerned and found the book. In the second case, the head of a middle school, after consultations with the teaching staff including the deputy-head, produced a modified timetable for the school. When the Head handed over a copy to the deputy-head for examination, the latter precipitately tore it into pieces and scattered them on the floor, shouting: 'It's no good, it won't do.'

Depicting structure – alternative forms

More than ever before schools may wish to present their structures on paper, perhaps for publicity purposes but especially for use by governing bodies and parental bodies. The foremost use, however, is certain to be within the staff itself. In trying to depict the structure of a school, teachers may find some satisfaction in using the pyramidal form, often called an organization chart. It provides certain information, but its limitations must be borne in mind. Among its deficiencies are the following:

- It cannot indicate the variation of work which an organization undertakes.
- No time-scale is given.
- It suggests only undimensional and vertical relations.
- The versatility of individuals is concealed.

An alternative form of depicting structure is known as the matrix. It makes good some of these deficiencies (Kingdon 1973). The use of the matrix presupposes a view of the task of the organization as ever-changing. Jobs, therefore, vary in duration, and may vary in kind. In teaching, it is not uncommon to find persons undertaking work that is quite different from that represented by their formal qualifications. It is true to say, however, that many forces in practice resist the level of organizational flexibility and personal adaptation which might be both desirable and attainable.

Where a fixed distribution of jobs, authority and positions is inappropriate and a variable structure is required, the matrix is a useful way of depicting the possibilities. Two fundamental ideas are necessary for devising a matrix.

1. The total curricular programme for the school as a whole must be conceived as ongoing but separable into any desired number of sub-programmes or courses of varying duration.

Curricular programme for the school
sub-programme for pupil year groups

Teams	1	2	3	4
Mathematics				
English				
Creative studies				
Investigative studies				

Figure 4.11 Example of matrix structure in a junior or middle school

2. The total staff available are sub-divided on any desired basis for the purpose of discharging the sub-programmes as analysed.

Since both the curriculum of a school and the staff available to teach it are subject to change, it is possible to construct a matrix in two ways.

Fixed teams – variable programmes. In this form of the matrix, the staff are divided into teams with fixed membership. Each team subscribes its expertise to two or more sub-programmes at any one time. In those circumstances, the work that the team does is limited to the expertise it possesses. The pupil, because of the limited composition of a team, might be expected to be exposed to the teaching of more than one team.

In a school for the age-range 8–12 an example of structure in matrix form (Figure 4.11) might be as follows. If only four teams comprehended all the curriculum between them, and the contribution of each was uniform throughout the school, the commitment of each team to each year group of pupils would be 25 per cent. In practice, all kinds of permutations may be considered and the final decisions entered in the boxes. For example, the Mathematics team might contribute 60 per cent of the work for 4, 20 per cent for 3, 10 per cent for 2 and 10 per cent for 1, whereas the Creative Studies team might contribute 20 per cent, 10 per cent, 10 per cent and 60 per cent respectively to the same pupil year groups. English might then contribute 10 per cent, 10 per cent, 60 per cent and 20 per cent with Investigative Studies contributing 10 per cent, 60 per cent, 20 per cent and 10 per cent respectively.

The matrix could be further applied to the working of any one of these teams alone. If the team had four members, the individual teachers would replace the teams in the matrix. In each box could be shown the contribution made by each in respect of all four pupil year-groups. Indeed, a more detailed analysis of the sub-programme for each of the year-groups would be needed.

Example Sub-programmes	The total staff available Variably formed teams according to need			
	1	2	3	4
Lower school Humanities programme				
Personal and Social Education programme				
GCSE programme				
GCE A Level programme				

Figure 4.12 Example of matrix structure in a secondary school

It may be noted that in schools where such teams are held to be omnicompetent and committed only to one year-group, the matrix is not needed. A simple pyramidal form is all that is required.

Fixed programmes – variable teams.   Being able to vary the composition of teams is a central consideration in using a matrix to depict structure, as shown in Fig. 4.12 for a secondary school. In this case, the sub-programmes may be conceived as relatively stable. The need is to form the very best teams possible and to vary the membership as necessary to maintain high standards or to bring to bear on a certain sub-programme the specialist contributions of a number of people. Each team would be subject to high-level overall leadership but various team members would lead the team's contribution to particular sub-programmes.

This particular matrix, if it applied to a secondary school, would imply two distinct differences from the traditional departmental structure. In the first place a team is specially formed for a purpose – to run a specific sub-programme. To do this it has far greater autonomy than that accorded to traditional departments. It is virtually an independent management unit. In the second place an individual teacher would be a member of different teams over a period of time, and a member of two teams simultaneously, perhaps, bearing in mind the need at all times to compose optimum teams in terms of balanced skills and cohesion.

The forms used to depict the structure of a school should be capable of portraying the part or the whole. The examples given in this chapter so far have confined themselves to the teaching staff and their curricular and pastoral work. An inclusive analysis of the school as an extended organization, however, should take into account many more factors. The matrix may be used for this purpose, as demonstrated in Figure 4.13, freely modified to allow the four sets of critical functions to be related. Inside the box, by means of different kinds of line, direct, indirect, strong

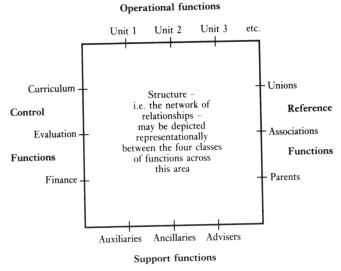

Figure 4.13 Matrix structure depicting whole-school functions

and weak relations may be shown, not only as between groups, but also, if enough detail is added, between individuals. Under operational functions, on the north side of the box, Units 1, 2, etc. refer to teams, departments or any other identifiable sub-groups for getting the work of the school actually discharged.

Between them they encompass all the teaching functions whether conceived as instructional alone, or 'academic' and 'administrative' as separable functions. Individuals are grouped according to mutual interests, qualifications and programme demands. On the south side of the box are the support functions. There may be grouped on a similar basis all those whose organizational functions are of a second order, but are vitally necessary to the effective operation of the school. On the west side of the box may be listed those people whose function is regulatory, grouped according to the various spheres where control must be exercised over the operational life of the school. Some examples are given as the curriculum, evaluation (pupil, teacher and organizational performance) and finance. The governors, the head and various senior staff would be grouped for each of these. On the east side of the box are grouped people – some known, some unknown as individuals – who act as reference groups in different ways to the teaching and non-teaching staff of the school. The parents are a powerful known group. Professional or trades unions and subject or professional associations, though not all in direct contact with a school, exercise normative influence by various means.

In thinking of the school in its entirety as an organization, six primary variables may be used to measure the structure and thus to make it possible to compare the structures of different schools (Pugh and Hickson 1976).

1. the degree of specialization of function; that is, the division of work;
2. the degree of standardization of procedures; that is, the existence of rules;
3. the degree of formalization of documentation; that is, the commitment of rules and other types of information to writing;
4. the degree of centralization of authority; that is, the location of decision making;
5. the configuration of positions; that is, the 'shape' which the structure assumes;
6. the flexibility of structure; that is, the capacity of structure to meet new conditions and accept new tasks.

Types of structure – theoretical extremes

Many efforts have been made to identify major principles which underlie the structures of organizations as found in practice. On the basis of such principles structures may then be classified. The principle of adaptation is one which has enduring interest and relevance to the work of the schools.

In *mechanistic* structures, the predominant condition is inflexibility. When the ends pursued by an organization are clearly perceived, stable in concept and unchanging in nature, the means which may be adopted for achieving the ends may correspondingly assume defined and predictable dimensions. Exactitude in the distribution of jobs, authority and positions may be achieved. A superordinate–subordinate principle may be clearly determined and made a central feature of structure. A chain of command binds the organization into a coherent, centrally directed whole. Communications pass through prescribed and orthodox channels. Initiative and diversity are minimized, since they are dispensed with by providing operating procedures for every eventuality.

In *organismic* or *organic* structures the opposite conditions prevail. The organization is conceived as trying to survive in constantly unstable and changing circumstances. At any point in time, the primary criterion for the distribution of jobs, authority and positions is making the best use of the human resources available, irrespective of precedence. The actual contributions of individuals and the pattern of interaction between individuals adopted must meet only the tests of possibility and suitability in relation to the task faced and the objectives set.

Mechanistic structure represents a closed value system
Organic structure represents an open value system

It may be argued that the type of structure actually found in schools reflects 'internal' factors, like objectives, resources and preferences, but also 'external' factors like the school's historical development, providing body, location and size, level of independence and the kind of socio-economic community it serves.

Above all else, perhaps, structure is determined by the technology of the school – the characteristic way in which it undertakes its work, determined by the nature of the work itself. When a school is very small, the work is controlled by personal contact. Individuals know their jobs, authority and positions implicitly. People are usually flexible in their working methods. Typically, as the school grows, the personal, on-the-job control of the teaching gives way to control through 'specialists' in the organization who have singular status. With further growth, there is increasing direction and less discretion, control by more specialists and laid-down procedures. Finally, the school will reach a state of high specialization, or fine division of work, with many formalized procedures supported by codes of regulations. As discussed in Chapter 2, organization maintenance costs may have become excessive by this time. A new ideology may be necessary to provide a fundamentally different and more economic structure.

The structure of the school, as a result of human decision and action, should be seen in relation to the large and often ill-defined stock of ideas which inspire and guide community life in general. The values cherished by the community as a whole permit and constrain specific arrangements within organization.

Size of organization is commonly a topic of concern and is often thought to be a critical variable in terms of engaging the 'whole person' in the work of the organization. Small organizations are often thought to be consistent with human happiness, efficiency and effectiveness. The criteria by which 'size' can be measured, however, vary and include numbers of people and financial and physical criteria such as the extent of buildings. Large organizations are often thought to be automatically malignant. The distinction should be drawn, however, between 'total' size and 'local' size. A multinational company may indeed be an enormous organization in total, but each operational sub-unit may be very small, intimate and satisfactory as a workplace.

By the same token, a school in total may seem of immense proportions, whatever criteria are adopted. This does not necessarily mean that such a school is a bad place to work in: a small school can be equally as bad. The structure adopted in any school needs to take account of the numbers of people involved, the task in hand, the technology adopted and the physical facilities and equipment available. Control, integration, flexibility and freedom from stress in an effective organization are the common objectives of all organizations, irrespective of size. Lack of understanding of alternative structures, or persistence with maladapted structures – as when there is great growth or great decline in the size of organization – are managerial deficiencies.

Organizational ideology and structure

Organizations cherish and demonstrate values in everything they do. Structure embodies prime values. Some of these values may be classified under the terms democracy, bureaucracy and federalism.

Democracy.   Democracy is sometimes assumed to be an indivisible means for solving organizational problems. There are numerous definitions of democracy and in practice it is difficult to obtain consensus as to its meaning and application in precise situations. Democracy is concerned with ends in that the actual decisions made should result only from a decision-making process which is shared by all those who are to be affected by those decisions. Thus, the primary factors in democracy are participation and consent. An important corollary is the right to disagree. Recognition must be given, therefore, to the principle of dissent. Since dissent may be very inconvenient in practice, however, it may be tempting to employ coercive measures against dissenters. It is necessary, therefore, to accept dissent with impunity. Dissent is by definition a minority position. In democracy, the minority must be respected but the minority in turn is expected to observe the majority decision and to support its implementation.

As a consequence, decisions are made and practical problems are tackled in an open atmosphere of dialogue in which minority opinion forms and attempts to influence enough opinion to become itself the majority view. The size of schools and sheer physical problems of assembly, communication and consumption of time are potentially inimical to the practice of democracy. Ways to overcome the difficulties, however, may be found.

In direct democracy, all the people concerned must meet for discussion and to make decisions. Any member should be able to raise any matter and identify it as a problem. In other words, the concerns of one are potentially the concerns of all.

In representative democracy, the people concerned are too numerous to meet as a group. Representatives are nominated to act for the group. If this person has full powers vested in him, as a plenipotentiary, then he is empowered to make decisions which the group he represents will automatically accept. Such a person in this case must clearly be the choice of the group concerned.

A delegate, however, may be assigned by the group to represent its views but without power to commit it to any decision. Both the plenipotentiary and the delegate are accountable to the group, which retains the right to withdraw the office.

Democracy in procedural terms must cope with the different abilities of the members of the group and the varying degrees of willingness to lead and to take office. The principle of election in the group may be used to determine leadership or office on a permanent basis, a prescribed temporary basis, a regular basis subject to efficiency or on a shared basis in which positions are rotated with agreed time intervals.

The numerous definitions of democracy all attempt to address a certain form of government of nation states or units of provincial or local government within them. Since the word 'government' is synonymous with management in the sense that a government in office is responsible for the management of the political unit concerned, it is feasible to expect that 'democracy' can apply to an individual organization within it, such as a school. But in practice the word is used by teachers and others in schools in a variety of ways. Sometimes it is used by way of appeal against directive regimes, at others to justify a particular course of action chosen or to condemn the way in which something has been done.

Democracy in the school may be viewed as both a *technical* process and a *psychological* process. The technical process includes concepts such as representation, election, majority decision, accountability, limited contract appointments, minority deviation, and competing ideology and policies. The psychological process includes concepts such as recognition of individual differences, respect for varying views, caring for individuals, freedom of speech, the opportunity to give or represent one's views, consultation, the reconciliation of varying interests and building decisions by negotiation. Whilst the psychological process can be implemented at will, the technical process has limited application in school. Pupils and students are compelled by law to attend until sixteen years of age. They do not elect their teachers who in turn do not elect the head and senior staff, although parent and teacher governors are subject to election. Accountability has become strengthened with the establishment of pupil profiling and staff appraisal. Majority decisions are common in staff meetings and meetings of school governors. Sub-groups of governors specifically formed to hear appeals from staff are in use. Limited appointments are in evidence in the case of incentive allowances but not in the case of substantive positions. Minority deviation and competing ideology and policies are regarded as antithetical to parental, community and school interests.

Bureaucracy. Bureaucracy is often viewed as the antithesis of democracy. If democracy places more emphasis on ends in order to determine what the means should be, bureaucracy reverses the emphasis. It is preoccupied with order, logic and efficiency. The natural and ineradicable inequality of individuals is a fact which must lead to a hierarchical arrangement of rights and obligations. Decision emanates from one or few to many. The ability and right to identify issues which call for decision is the prerogative of one or few in any organization.

Organization members are not expected to concern themselves with the organization as a whole. There are different levels of concern, at each of which decision-making is in limited hands. Decisions actually made are dependent on prior decision made at superordinate level and which, in turn, strictly affect those subsequently made at subordinate level. There is, therefore, a defined chain of command and communication. Jobs, authority and positions are prescribed, delegated and regulated.

Rules and procedures control all eventualities which may arise over the work to be done. In theory, novel events and problems should be anticipated at the very highest levels. In any case, novel circumstances should be referred from subordinate to superordinate levels. The division of labour is fine and the individual's concern is to maintain the *status quo*. Promotion is based upon his ability to do so rather than on eccentric flair and influence.

Like democracy, as a concept bureaucracy is not indivisible. It is identified in practice as a variable phenomenon, though in the past it was regarded as a homogeneous tool which would have to be used by all organizations in the modern technological society. Apologists have pointed out just how much has in fact been achieved by the application of bureaucracy, but have shown that variations in the modes of application can have varying effects – to the great harm as well as to the benefit of an organization (Gouldner 1955; Blau 1956).

Federalism. Federalism as a principle may be seen as lying mid-way between democracy and bureaucracy. It avoids the completely open position postulated by democracy in which decision-making is decentralized and the course of an organization is in theory unpredictable. It also avoids the directive approach and highly predictable outcomes sought in bureaucracy.

In an organization, participation is both possible and desirable in the making of decisions concerning some ends and some means. The possibility of constant, fundamental reappraisals generated by democracy and the inertia and potential maladaptability of bureaucracy are both avoidable. Flexibility and creativity can be secured by a process of deliberate and comprehensive decentralization. This is achieved by the constant and constitutional act of devolving responsibility from the centre to the periphery in an organization.

At the centre of the structure, the task of defining the nature of the organization's work is undertaken, together with an appraisal of the total and quality of resources available. In addition, the recruitment, induction and maintenance of the organization's membership is decided there. A small number of major prerogatives are, therefore, handled at the centre. The deployment of resources and the management of actual operations may then be fully devolved on sub-groups which, within the framework of possibilities created, are then deemed autonomous.

Organizational structure therefore can be thought of as the distribution of jobs, authority and positions among the members of an organization. In a school, the structure may be regarded and depicted in two basic forms. The pyramidal form is a common way of representing structure. It articulates fixed positions and prescribed subordinate–superordinate relations, but does not provide for change. The matrix, in contrast, stresses the changing nature of the work and various combinations of staff which may be arranged to discharge it.

Structures in practice range between two extreme theoretical types. 'Mechanistic' structures are an adaptation to stable working conditions and tasks. 'Organismic' structures are adaptations to changing conditions and tasks. A way of measuring structure may consist of using six primary variables: specialization, standardization, formalization, centralization, configuration and flexibility.

Structure in practice

The terms democracy, bureaucracy and federalism reflect different values. Each has a different bearing on the kind of structure a school might seek and the actual features which are adopted. An effective structure is one that gives life and health to the organization, enabling it to reach its objectives with efficiency. It can be detected in the manifest well-being of organization members. By the opposite token, the ineffective structure can be detected when organization members are less than positive about their work. The evidence either way takes the form of a myriad of possible signs. The following is a list of typical examples in the negative mode.

> 'The feeling that you have too little authority to carry out responsibilities assigned to you.'
> 'Being unclear on just what the scope and responsibilities of your job are.'

'Feeling that you have too heavy a work load, one that you can't possibly finish during an ordinary work day.'

'Thinking that you are not able to satisfy the conflicting demands of various people over you.'

'Feeling that you are not fully qualified to handle the job.'

'Feeling you are unable to influence your immediate supervisor's decisions and actions that affect you.'

'Feeling that you have to do things on the job that are against your better judgement.'

(Wheeler 1971:3)

Conscious of the need to review the structure, one local education authority once formally reminded heads of schools to ask themselves from time to time if their awareness of the actual working loads being carried by individual teaching and non-teaching members of staff was up to date and accurate.

A structure which is ineffective means that people are not doing their jobs properly for one reason or another. The causes for this may lie within the powers of the individual or it may be attributable to management, though the dividing line between the two is not as clear cut as may appear at first sight. Those which lie within the control of the individual for the most part include:

- accidents
- absence
- poor time-keeping
- careless workmanship
- idleness
- choice of wrong methods
- non-observance of required procedures
- failure to be informed

Those which lie within the control of management for the most part include

- bad planning and programming
- insufficient or unstandardized procedures
- lack of specification of jobs, authority and position
- poor information systems
- excessive innovation
- too many incomplete projects
- unsatisfactory working conditions
- insufficient materials and equipment

Structure is effective when organization members are enabled to give their best and reach their objectives. Having significant numbers of members who are not giving their best is an ever-present possibility but one which is to be avoided. It seems that some people work from inner principle and can ride external difficulties and discouragements more than others who depend far more on external conditions for stimulation and direction. Particular attention needs to be given to the latter. It is possible for those most subject to external conditions to drift slowly into alienation or even into pathological states involving varying degrees of mental and physical suffering. In recent years the word 'stress' has become common currency for referring to any unwelcome personal condition ranging from mild disenchantment to life-threatening psychological burdens, which are rightly or wrongly attributed to being at work and thereby spring from the structure which governs the individual's contribution at work. But stress may also arise at home or originate elsewhere in an individual's private life so that the focus usually needs to be on the identification of a deleterious mix to the detriment of performance at work and happiness at home. Action to counter stress typically works to establish what the stressers are, the individual's perceptions of them, responses made to them and the consequences for the individual as a basis for remedial treatment.

Caring for people at work is tantamount to trying to relieve stress. Its milder forms may be met with counselling and other forms of first-aid but in the end structural changes may be necessary such as a change of job content. Such caring is both a moral and an economic necessity but usually presumes that those cared for are innocent victims whereas in the political life of an organization stress may often be self-inflicted, irrespective of the organizational structure. Nevertheless, the dimensions and nature of the structure can be altered to increase or decrease stress levels, particularly to avoid the 'burnout' of individuals by overwork and wastage of staff through dissatisfaction.

An important determining principle in this regard is whether to fit the job to the individual or the individual to the job. The first approach recognizes individual differences and makes concessions to them, avoiding *standard* measures and expectations, pay and promotion. The second approach recognizes the need to close the gap between the individual and the job to be done by exercising coercion or giving support and extra training.

Those who are in senior positions and take on a concern for the stress in others need to remember that they themselves are within the same structure they have created and may also become the victims of stress. Stress in the manager becomes a potent source of stress in others in many cases. The ability to recognize one's own work-load, fractious relationships and perhaps an unhappy private life as a potential cause of trouble for oneself and others is at a premium. An elaborate and ingenious study of a head at work, using a plethysmograph worn by the head and connected to a small transmitter which relayed signals to a receiver connected to a Tissue Perfusion Monitor, showed the vicissitudes of stress during the working day matched with the range of duties undertaken. On analysis ways could be found to make positive outweigh negative experiences, which means having a better coping strategy (Whan 1988).

Stress levels in teaching have almost certainly risen in recent years as schools have become more exposed to the vicissitudes of powerful external forces with jobs becoming more unpredictable with respect to their content and more complex and demanding as solutions to operational problems become more elusive and partial in a turbulent environment. Even so it remains that teaching is probably not among the most stressful occupations. The symptoms that appear in teaching are similar to those which appear in other occupations, ranging from persistent irritability through to increased drinking and smoking, a variety of physical disabilities and finally to heart attacks. Such outcomes in teaching have been listed as follows.

'A reaction of the nervous system to stress, leading to a variety of physical diseases.'
'A disruption of personal or professional life as a result of occupational stress.'
'Destructive feelings of emotional stress as a result of ineffective coping.'
'Loss of concern and detachment from those with whom you work.'
'A cynical and dehumanized perception of pupils, accompanied by a deterioration of the quality of teaching.'

(Walsh 1979)

In this context it needs to be remembered that pupils too may experience stress. This can arise from teacher conduct, peer group conduct, workload or parental pressure and expectation.

The adage that prevention is better than cure applies to stress as to many other matters. Dunham (1989) has long argued that stress is the name for the negative outcome or condition resulting from an imbalance between demands or claims made on the individual by others or which he or she makes on himself or herself and the availability of resources commanded by the individual to meet them. In reverse, with too many resources to hand and little demand being made on them, the individual may then experience frustration or boredom which in turn may become stressful.

The ideal condition at any time is having a nice balance between the demands made of an individual and that individual's ability to meet them with a reasonable degree of comfort. That is to supply the intellect, energy, time and talent needed. It is a common experience that demands build up more quickly than the ability to meet them. Disproportionate attempts are then made to satisfy these demands and a pathological condition then ensues. To avoid this, coping resources need to be employed involving any device which has value to the particular individual concerned as a counterweight to these demands. Such devices may range from stamp collecting to meditation, from jogging to moonlighting.

It is inferred from this that a constant audit needs to be made by which the individual reviews the demands made on him or her and the range of coping devices or resources which can be brought to bear by the individual to meet them. This may be especially necessary with rapid promotion. Following a self-audit it may well be necessary deliberately to build in coping behaviours which distract, refresh and re-energize.

The wider community offers inumerable opportunities which can be used as coping devices. The structure itself may be a source of support. If the climate is right and the leadership suitable, the sub-group such as a departmental staff group or the staff of a small school as a whole can prevent the individual from feeling isolated and make it possible for him or her to survive a difficult period and go on to cope successfully with the job.

5 *Managing for results*

The idea of management is not restricted to formal organizations. It applies to the family, the nation, the international community and the human environment at large. When people speak of parents as being incompetent they usually mean that the parents manage their family affairs badly. Similarly the affairs of the national community can be either well or badly managed, as can relations between different national communities. In recent times people everywhere have become conscious of the fact that the common natural environment upon which the existence of the human species depends is itself subject to bad or good management.

Survival and order are characteristic notions embedded in all these cases, bearing in mind the need to think about the long-term future as well as the immediate. It is inadequate, however, to confine the meaning of management simply to a measure of success. There is the paradox that good management is exhibited in many conditions of apparent failure or disaster. The winding up of a company, a military retreat, a disaster at sea, a massive reduction in rail services or a widespread closure of pits in the coal-mining industry may all be well or badly managed.

If an adjective must be found to indicate the desirable state of management, that word is 'effective'. Management is human behaviour and it is effective when human needs embodied in objectives are met. In essence, therefore, management is the organizational process of formulating objectives, acquiring and committing the resources required to reach them and ensuring that the objectives are actually reached. It is a process of matching objectives and resources and is ultimately a *social* process. In this process objectives may have to be limited to the resources which are available or it may be necessary to procure resources to make it possible to attain the desired objectives. In this context 'good' management is obtaining exceptional results (objectives) with unexceptional resources – particularly if this is achieved in unpropitious circumstances.

At any point in time an organization has a particular status or location in a life cycle, as shown in Figure 5.1. Reading from left to right, the organization in general terms has an upward direction. Parts of it may be deficient or even failing but the overall condition of the organization is

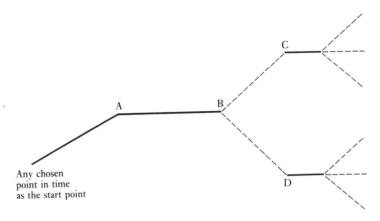

Figure 5.1 The Life Cycle of an Organisation

one of prosperity and achievement. Its members feel that everything is going well. The strategic task for management is to keep the direction going – to sustain the general slope. Once this momentum is lost a plateau develops, as at Point A. There are no new initiatives, perhaps important assets are lost and members feel a loss of enthusiasm and confidence.

The challenge for management emerges at Point B. The organization may be rescued with a resumption of an upward direction to Point C or it may go into actual decline to Point D. At Points C and D a plateau may set in, representing a lesser achievement in the case of Point C but a greater achievement of management in the case of Point D.

Thereafter the three dimensions can variously appear – the upward slope, the plateau and the downward slope. Many factors will govern which one applies. There may well be factors beyond the control of the school, such as the loss of local population, the announcement of a future date for the closure of the school, a serious fire or the sudden death in post of a key person. But given normal and reasonable conditions the school can be given its directions in terms of the figure by the collective action of its management.

Management and schools

The use of the term management in educational vocabulary is of comparatively recent origin. Its use has been controversial and sometimes acrimonious. The main reason for this is that the interpretations given to the word have been very limited and coloured by the meanings which people in education think are given to the word in manufacturing and commerce, and by the practice of management which they think exists there.

> The characterization of the practice of management traditionally was in rather formal and simplistic terms and it is easier now to diagnose its limitations. It tended to be based on an inadequate understanding of individual and group behaviour, an insensitivity to social considerations, excessive division of labour, serious difficulties in and handling of authority relationships and in keeping a reasonable measure of control whilst not undermining the creative and initiating capacities of people. Newer thinking is providing better concepts for understanding the motivation and behaviour of people and for designing organizations in the light of this knowledge, an improved capacity to analyse and assess conflicting pressures, a greater acknowledgement of the factors of uncertainty and risk-taking in the policy and decision making responsibilities of management, a capacity to understand problems which cannot be neatly compartmented, a recognition that the integration of effort and activities is an infinitely more difficult yet more vital process than the processes of subdivision and specialisation.
>
> (Brodie 1979:1–2)

Management is concerned with both objective and subjective phenomena. A great deal of the misunderstanding in education arises because people think of management as being concerned *only* with the objective – with measuring output and being accountable on the basis of measurable results. That this is only part of the matter is well illustrated in the following passage.

> Because management deals with human beings, it can never be completely scientific, and must be regarded partly as an art. The reason for this is that while scientific techniques are applied to materials governed by known physical laws, the techniques of management are applied to people and must rely on people to ensure that they are properly applied. They can only be successfully applied by someone who has learned to understand people by experience of dealing with them.
>
> (International Labour Office 1964:26)

Management involves values, attitudes, techniques and behavioural patterns at both strategic and tactical levels. All these, however, do not constitute an indivisible whole which may be either accepted or rejected. They are varying in nature and are as much a part of the infinite variety of reality as anything else. Different types of organization call for different types of management, different situations within a particular organization require specific skills. The realization that organization in education should be properly managed is incumbent on everyone, as stated in the following quotation.

> Management and its techniques are applicable at all levels of the educational service and I mean *all levels* because it doesn't matter whether you are a

class teacher or head of department, or a head teacher or an administrative officer in local government or even a civil servant, there are management techniques which are appropriate to your particular sphere of activity.

(Brooksbank 1972:9)

It is reasonable to differ over the *quality* of management which is exercised but there can be no question about the *existence* of management and the *need* for it in educational institutions. Wherever there is organization there is management. Management is to organization as the skin is to the body. In practical terms, schools share the fate of other organizations in adult life. Some are well managed: they are judged useful for social purposes and their members enjoy their membership of the organizations concerned as a way of spending their working life. Some are badly managed: they are judged harshly because their work is of ill-repute and their members are alienated or even hostile. Every conceivable gradation between these two extremes may be found.

Management is complex human activity whether the viewpoint is that of an individual person in action or that of a group of people in action as a management team. Many attempts to classify all the behaviour involved have been made. All of them are concerned to analyse the functions which are necessary if an organization is to survive and prosper. An example of such an analysis is that of planning, regulating, commanding, coordinating, controlling and evaluating (Urwick 1963). In essence, however, management is being concerned with a series of simple but unavoidable questions, which apply equally when the scale of organization and the resources used is large as well as small. These questions may be arranged as follows.

PURPOSE	**What** is done?
	Why is it done?
	What **else** might be done?
	What **should** be done?
PLACE	**Where** is it done?
	Why is it done **there**?
	Where **else** might it be done?
	Where **should** it be done?
SEQUENCE	**When** is it done?
	Why is it done **then**?
	When **might** it be done?
	When **should** it be done?
PERSON	**Who** does it?
	Why does **that** person do it?
	Who **else** might do it?
	Who **should** do it?

Applied fields / Individual skills	Educational	External relations	Finance and facilities	Staff development
Conceptual				
Technical				
Human				

Figure 5.2 School management model based on individual skills and applied fields (Adapted from a talk by W. Taylor, 'A Working Partnership', BBC Radio, 1970)

MEANS   **How** is it done?
           Why is it done **that** way?
           How **else** might it be done?
           How **should** it be done?
                              (International Labour Office 1978:101–20)

The answer to these questions and the ways and means used to find them will vary between schools. The history, size, type and catchment area of the school are some of the variables which affect the particular answers given. Over time, new answers to the old questions must be found and this requires ability, effort and constant vigilance. Management work is demanding. The school which runs smoothly may convey the misleading impression that it is easy work, whereas the school which moves from crisis to crisis may create the impression that good management is impossible to achieve.

Good management is obtaining exceptional results with unexceptional resources particularly when achieved in unpropitious circumstances.

School management models

The scope and task of management in the school are represented in the three models which follow. In the first of these the range of necessary skills in the individual is analysed and the major areas to which they may be applied are identified. This may be called the Applied Skills Model, presented as Figure 5.2. In this model *conceptual skills* are those of comprehensive understanding, the ability to integrate all the elements involved, the ability to perceive possibilities and to relate events to higher order principles. *Technical skills* are those of 'know-how', the possession of information, motor and behavioural competences, knowledge of procedures and the constraints and resources which govern the work of a school together with specific techniques. *Human skills* are those of being able to encourage people to give their best efforts to the organization, to create a healthy climate of working conditions, to introduce changes without losing morale and to communicate clearly and in such a manner as to create confidence.

All these skills are needed and may be exhibited in each of the four applied fields. The *educational* field includes the curricular programme, its objectives, syllabus content and coordination, and the teaching methods and techniques employed. The field of *external relations* includes creating and sustaining a favourable image of the school in the minds of parents, the media, the many agencies which have an interest in the school, local government officers and other officials, and local firms and bodies which may be of service to the school. The field of *finance and facilities* covers all the non-human resources which are available to the school, particularly the use of plant. The field of *staff development* includes the matching of person to job, performance evaluation, redeployment and the progressive increase of staff competences.

The second model of management in the school turns on the notion of the range of decisions which must be made and the patterns of participation by which they are made. This may be called the Participation Model, presented as Figure 5.3.

The nominated items under *decision areas* represent a set of categories for sorting all the decisions which are made in the course of managing the school. They are derived from conceptualizing the complete spectrum of decisions which a school must make. Suitable analytical divisions of this spectrum are then made and appropriately labelled. This particular set is not inviolable but is an attempt to encompass every conceivable decision. This means that the labels must be interpreted broadly.

'Curriculum content' covers decisions to choose and reject the content of the learning programme. This includes subject identification on the academic side but also decisions on questions of an interdisciplinary approach, project activity and individualized programmes, insofar as learning method and experience become content, and the materials to be used for teaching the chosen content.

'Educational objectives' are thought of as changes hoped for in the pupils as a result of having followed the programme offered by the school – including the process of defining these changes, modifying them, publishing them or, in short, arriving at any shared, explicit conclusion or statement about what the work of the school is for.

Participation Levels / Decision Areas	Decisional deprivation	Decisional equilibrium	Decisional saturation
Curriculum content			
Educational objectives			
Evaluation			
External relations			
Finance			
Pupil grouping			
Staffing			
Teaching methods/ techniques			
Timetabling/ use of plant			
Use of materials/ equipment			

Figure 5.3 School management model based on decision areas and participation levels

'Evaluation' indicates the area of decision concerned with the design and extent of pupil records of achievement and the choice of any diagnostic and/or predictive tests to be used. This category also includes procedures to be adopted by the teachers and questions such as the accessibility of various parties to the records. Finally, it embraces all decisions regarding measures of teacher performance and organizational effectiveness, together with decisions on the procedures and arrangements for making use of them.

'External relations' includes all contacts for whatever purpose with a parent or guardian in connection with the pupil's work, relationships or conduct and condition. This includes documentary contact such as the sending of written information and reports, replying to letters, and requesting parental visits to school for advisory or consultative purposes. In addition, this category includes all decisions about relations with external bodies of all kinds, the local authority, the mass media and the school's neighbours.

The decision area labelled 'finance' refers to all discretionary monies available to the school. It includes questions of disbursement – the actual amounts which individuals or groups receive, whether or not this is paid in a lump sum for autonomous expenditure, and whether or not any direction is attached to agreed grants. This decision area involves expenditure on staffing, building services, equipment and material. In short, this category is concerned with all incoming and outgoing monies in various forms, uses to which they are put and procedures for handling them under local financial management.

The category 'pupil grouping' stands for the complete process of sub-grouping of the total pupil population of the school, together with group recompositions and modifications. It includes the bases for sub-groupings, their size and degree of permanence and the level of discretion over sub-sub-grouping by the individual teacher, teaching team, department or faculty.

'Staffing' includes appointments, deployment, promotions, retraining and development, working hours, the assignment of student teachers and all matters to do with the adult members of the organization as employees, insofar as they lie within the powers of discretion afforded to the school.

'Teaching methods/techniques' involves how the individual teacher or teaching team goes about his or its work. It includes the division of labour between teachers, the type of division of labour between teacher and pupil and between pupils, and the regulatory behaviour employed by the staff. This also includes questions of quality, quantity, sequence and pace of the pupil's work, the particular way chosen to teach a particular content and coping with learning difficulties and indiscipline.

'Timetabling/use of plant' stands for the adopted programme of activities or learning experiences and involves the allocation of plant and facilities, the amount of time devoted to any particular unit of curriculum, the times when rooms and facilities may be used, the use that may actually be made of them, subsequent changes in their use and what plant and facilities are permanently allocated or rationed on a time basis.

The 'use of materials/equipment' refers to consumable and non-consumable items needed for teaching purposes by teachers and/or the pupils. Questions of kind, quality and quantity are included, as are questions of storage, mode of distribution and actual usage.

The term *participation* in the model refers to the amount of decision-making which individuals are empowered to undertake. It is not uncommon to hear assertions that one person – notably the head of school – makes all the decisions. Such assertions are patently unfounded. It is true, however, that some decisions are more important and far reaching for the life of the school than others. These decisions often remain in the hands of the head of school or the governors or in the hands of a few members of the teaching staff. Given such a list of decision areas in the model, it is possible to assign an order of priority to each in terms of its strategic importance to the overall life of the school. Furthermore, it is possible for individuals in the organization to assess the amount of say which they feel they have in each area. This will reveal either a state of satisfaction or *decisional equilibrium*, a state of unsatisfied demand or *decisional deprivation*, or a state of overwork or *decisional saturation* (Alutto and Belasco 1972).

> Members of an organization experience a sense of either decisional deprivation
> (desired participation is in excess of actual participation)
> or
> decisional equilibrium
> (desired participation and actual participation are equal)
> or
> decisional saturation
> (actual participation is in excess of desired participation)

Original authority lies with the person appointed as head of school, together with the governing body whose powers and duties are now greater than ever before and sanctioned in law. In practice the governing body may dominate the head. In contrast the head might dominate the governing body. But, in general, gradations of harmonious working relationships exist whereby the head's authority derives its strength from a supportive and facilitative governing body. One of the most important manifestations and applications of this authority is to decide on the levels of participation which the school as an organization shall have. In general, the head may strive for high or low levels of participation. In addition, high levels of participation may be confined to a small proportion of staff or extended to all. These levels may apply to all decision areas or only to some of them. The actual pattern of participation deriving from the interplay of all these variables in a particular school forms the basis for a staff development policy and obviously a point of departure for a management strategy to increase or reduce the extent of decision-making powers.

In schools which have intermediate authority levels, such as team leaders, heads of department and heads of year groups, the participation policy favoured by the head of school may or may not be faithfully reflected within the sub-organization – though generally in teaching, as elsewhere, 'people lower down tend to take their attitudes from the man at the top' (International Labour Office 1978:38).

The ability and willingness to work in accordance with the general policy is of course a factor governing the selection of teachers for middle management positions in many schools. Some schools prefer to have a homogeneous character for their organization in regard to participation, leaning either to restricted or to extended levels of participation. Others may deliberately choose to be heterogeneous, in which case sub-organizations are allowed to run their affairs in their own way.

As the foregoing considerations imply, it is a fact that people differ in the ways in which they want to approach their managerial tasks. Heads of schools and senior teachers in all kinds of positions exhibit different behaviour as they go about their work. The principles underlying these differences are important and have differential effects on organizational performance. Personal behaviour in managerial work is known as management 'style', exhibited by individuals or by a formal group such as a senior management team.

The third school management model may be based on staff development needs. Since the staff is a principal asset, any changes to it are important, particularly qualitative changes. Management can adopt varying degrees of indifference to the qualitative improvement of staffing or it can actively seek to promote it, which is really what is meant by having a staff development policy. In this model the entire management of the school is analysed into ten areas on one side of a matrix, the other side being occupied by different groups of staff analysed according to circumstances and need. If formal positions are used to group them, they could consist of governors, senior management staff, middle management staff, other staff and non-teaching staff. The object is to form a picture of the levels of current staff awareness and expertise with a view to updating or improving it as needed in the light of changes within the school and external to the school which have already arrived or are anticipated. Whole sub-groups may need updating or retraining as occurred with the introduction of the National Curriculum. The model is presented as Figure 5.4.

Management Area / Staff Group	Governors	Senior Management Staff	Middle Management Staff	Other Teaching Staff	Non-Teaching Staff
Physical Assets					
School Climate					
Values and Objectives					
Curriculum Content and Development					
Organization, Care and Development of Pupils					
Staff Structure and Deployment					
Financial and Systems Management					
Standards of Performance					
External Relations					
Management Skills					

Figure 5.4 School management model based on staff development needs

Sharing management work

It is far too simplistic to think that the larger the school the greater the amount of management activity and the higher the level of difficulty. To a considerable extent the amount of management work required is in the hands of the organization itself. A small school may be highly complex as an organization and require a great deal of managing. A large school may be less complex as an organization and require less managing. In both cases the volume of management activity required may be undertaken by one person or few, or it may be shared widely. If a school is organized in a less complex way it may be possible for the head of school or a few senior staff to undertake all the important managerial behaviour, though it may be undesirable for them to do so. For one person or few to manage a complex organization, however, is really a contradiction of terms. More complexity means more interpersonal transactions, the sheer volume of which needs a broader or decentralized management base.

The process of delegation is an inevitable consequence of finite human capacity facing the extending complexity of organization. The infinite welter of stimuli which clamour for attention in organizations must be limited, filtered and shared. At any point in time the experience and ability of each member enables him to share a certain part of the organization's total burdens but this part is limited for every individual. Each is unable to respond to additional stimuli beyond a certain limit.

> No head can exercise leadership without delegating most of his responsibilities. But he may delegate in a number of ways. He may delegate responsibility but not the power; he may delegate the task but not the power; he may delegate the power but not the accountability. In each of these cases his delegations would be dysfunctional in that the teacher would not be able to perform the delegated task fully and would remain in a state of subordination or dependency which would be restrictive of future initiatives. A more useful management concept is that of collaboration or sharing – which is true 'delegation'. Collaboration involves total sharing of responsibilities which includes the right to succeed and to fail. There can be no real sharing (delegation) if the right to fail is not also shared (delegated) since anything less is incomplete and cannot be said to be true sharing (delegation). A head who does not share (delegate) the right to fail may be retaining control over the situation but he cannot be said to be showing full respect for and confidence in his colleagues. A vital consideration for all managers is the extent to which they dare share their responsibilities – the assumption being that the stronger the individual the more he will risk. Generally speaking managers are paid to take risks even if they are calculated ones. Unless responsibilities and power are shared among the members the organization will lack creativity and adaptability. If schools are to be open, creative and supportive institutions for the pupils, they must be so for the teachers also.
>
> (Gray 1979:63)

Two special points about delegation need to be made. In the first place, it must be emphasized that delegation should be conceived as a continuous process. The *volume* of responsibilities which may be involved is always changing in total. The *kind* of responsibilities which may be subject to delegation over a period of time may change significantly in nature. Above all, however, the volume and kind of responsibilities which a particular individual at any particular time is asked to bear may be *decreased* as well as increased. Responsibilities may cease or may be moved from one person to another.

The second point concerns the fact that delegation is nearly always thought about as a hierarchical function. Delegation is often restricted in organizational thinking to the right and duty which a 'superordinate' or boss may exercise in relation to a 'subordinate'. The process of delegation at heart is a process of sharing management work. When a collegial – rather than a single hierarchical – principle governs the relationships between organization members, the process of sharing may be initiated by many people, all of whom may find themselves at the head of a hierarchy according to different task allocations and different circumstances. Thus, the 'subordinate' in one set of circumstances or for one particular task may be the 'superordinate' in another. This consideration underlies the final sentence in the passage quoted above.

Of the main zones of concern to those who manage the school, the academic and teaching zone involving the teaching staff is inevitably managed on a broad basis, through faculties, departments, year groups or teams, and individual teachers who have considerable autonomy in what they do and how they respond to the ever changing pattern of the school day. The involvement of teaching staff in the other zones of school life away from the immediate instructional and disciplinary situation, however, is a matter of great variability from school to school.

It is often forgotten that the non-teaching staff of a school are also members of the organization. They too are potentially able to undertake varying degrees of involvement in deciding on courses of action and helping to shape the kind of organization to which they belong.

> In all institutions little or no regard seems to be given to the views of the non-teaching staff. Their influence on policy is usually through the greater or lesser degree of co-operation with which they are prepared to receive the decisions of others. Yet the administrative, caretaking, clerical and catering staff can often be as large as the teaching staff and in ensuring the well-being and effectiveness of the community, as important.
>
> (Taylor 1975:5)

Management style

Management style has been briefly defined as the chosen behavioural strategy of an individual which he tends to repeat. In referring to the managerial behaviour of individuals in organizations, confusion between the terms 'strategy' and 'style' may arise. This confusion may be avoided, however, if a distinction is made between the two on the basis of the *intentions* of the individual manager concerned. The term 'strategy' is best reserved for the behavioural pattern which the individual chooses, implements and sustains in order to achieve the qualitative results he seeks. The term 'style' is best reserved for the impact *actually made on others*. Thus, 'style' is the visible aspect of strategy and depends upon the perceptual capacities of the receiver or observer of the managerial behaviour exhibited. The management style of a senior teacher, therefore, is the assessment made by colleagues in a particular work setting, based on sufficient observations of his working in a variety of circumstances.

> The management style of an individual may be defined as the characteristic way in which he goes about his managerial tasks in a specific organization assessed over the longer term by those who work with him

Since management is concerned in the final analysis with what organization members *are* doing, what they *might* be doing and what they *should* be doing, it is axiomatic that the basis of management is a set of general assumptions about people in organizations. These have been codified under two heads. The first set, known as 'Theory X', is pessimistic in tone. Those who take a 'Theory X' position expect little from the generality of people in terms of creative capacity, ability to make intelligent decisions, reliability and hard work without the application of sanctions. The second set, known as 'Theory Y', is optimistic in tone. Those who take a 'Theory Y' position expect much from others, believing in their creative capacity, participative willingness and potential reliability and application to work, given the right contextual conditions in the organization (McGregor 1960; 1967). It has been argued that the variable adoption of 'Theory X' and 'Theory Y' behaviour is possible and that it might be desirable in order to be fully adaptive. This formula has been named 'Theory Z' (Simmons 1971) and may be applied in organizations at three levels – at the level of the individual, at the level of the sub-group and at the level of the organization as a whole.

One manifestation of 'Theory X' is seen in the autocratic behaviour of the individual who enforces his own pre-determined decision by manipulative means which compel alienative or calculative responses in others. Another is seen in the efforts of the individual to gain acceptance of his own pre-determined decision by intellectual or emotive arguments. These constitute a form of duplicity in that they are attended by information-seeking and problem-explaining exercises which create the illusion that consultation or participation is taking place. A third manifestation of 'Theory X' is seen in the practice of consulting individuals on the subject of personal implications that might result from a decision made. In this way the support of a majority for an intended decision is amassed by the process of pre-empting hostility on grounds of guaranteed personal safeguards.

A manifestation of 'Theory Y' is seen in the practice of genuine delegation to appropriate sub-groups whose majority decisions are accepted and implemented. The individual who possesses the power to delegate plays no part in the proceedings. An important variant of this is also based on 'Theory Y'. The person with the power to delegate simply identifies the problem for the appropriate group and then participates personally in free discussion until a consensus or majority opinion is established.

A number of models have been created to capture the full range of possibilities indicated above. All of them depend in one form or another upon a two-factor theory. The two factors are emphasis on production – the impersonal dimension – and emphasis on morale – the personal dimension. Success turns inevitably upon the blend, but the case for an equal emphasis in *both* has been reinforced by empirically established findings. These include sources as diverse as heavy industry and schools – namely that work output is highest when managerial behaviour has a high equal impact in both dimensions (Misumi and Tasaki 1965; Paisey 1975).

One management style model uses the terms 'job-centred' and 'employee-centred' behaviour and identifies four 'systems' of behaviour in practice (Likert 1961; 1967). *System 1* is authoritarian and coercive. Decisions are made at the top and and communication is downward. The 'distance' between superior and subordinate is maximized. *System 2* is authoritative but benevolent with a good deal of subservience. Overt rewards are prominent, there is some delegation and communication is shaped to be received upwards. *System 3* is consultative, also with overt rewards. There are occasional punishments and some involvement in setting objectives and the choice of method. Communications are reciprocal but guarded for upward consumption. *System 4* features participative group management, with wide involvement in setting objectives and choosing methods. Economic rewards are available and communication is free and frank in all directions. Decision-making proceeds on a group basis and there is interlocking membership of groups.

A second model expresses the two factors in terms of 'concern for production' and 'concern for people'. A grid may be formed in which the former is the horizontal axis and the latter the vertical axis. In the 1.1 position lies 'impoverished management', bereft of both concern for people and concern for production. Effective production is unobtainable. People are lazy, apathetic and disengaged. At the interpersonal level, conflict is an ever present threat and relationships are destructive of human personality. In the 1.9 position – low for production, high for people – lies 'country-club management'. The preservation of social solidarity is the overriding consideration even at the expense of production. The confrontation of problems is delayed and escalating difficulties may be concealed beneath a veneer of mutual admiration, excessive familiarity and rationalization.

The opposite extreme to 'country-club management' is that of 'task management' in the 9.1 position, which is high for production, low for people. Human foibles and frailties are dismissed peremptorily in favour of rigid subordination and discipline. People and machines alike are programmed to fit with precision into arrangements which are planned and controlled with inexorable objectivity. The 5.5 position in the middle of the grid represents a management which alternates between giving attention to people and attention to production. This is the 'pendulum management', devoid of conviction and opportunist in style. The ideal is 'team management', which is simultaneously high in concern for production and people. This is the 9.9 position which achieves production with and through people who enjoy their work in a participative structure. It allows the demands of the task and the individual to integrate and to be met simultaneously (Blake and Mouton 1978).

A third model of management style uses the terminology 'task orientation' and 'relationships oritentation' to refer to the two factors. Four theoretical styles may be identified: separated; related; dedicated; and integrated. The *separated* category is reserved for individuals who are cautious, careful, conservative and orderly. They appear to prefer paper work, procedures and facts and look for established principles. They are accurate, precise, correct and perfectionist. They are steady, deliberate, patient, calm, modest and discreet. Behaviourally such individuals like to examine, administer, control and maintain. In the *related* category, people are valued and their personal development sought. Individuals in this category appear to be informal, quiet and to go unnoticed. They enjoy long conversations and are sympathetic, approving, accepting, friendly and anxious to create a secure atmosphere for others. In their behaviour they prefer to trust, to listen, to accept, to advise and to encourage.

In the *dedicated* category, individuals are determined, aggressive, confident, busy, driving and initiating. Tasks, responsibilities and standards are conceived at the individual rather than the group level. There is an emphasis on self-reliance, independence and ambition. Rewards, punishments and control are used in a context which stresses the primacy of task. In their behaviour, such people are oriented to organizing, initiating, directing, completing and evaluating. In the *integrated* category, individuals derive their authority from agreed aims, ideals, goals and policies. They value the integration of the individual and the organization and they work for greater participation and low power-differentials. They prefer shared objectives and responsibilities and study the more subtle forms of motivating others to work. Their behavioural pattern is directed towards achieving participation, interaction, motivation, integration and innovation.

In theory, actual organizational members can be grouped into these four categories. In practice they are found to lean either towards being *effective* or *ineffective* in their managerial behaviour. Thus, each of the four theoretical categories finds expression in both 'more effective' and 'less effective' forms. Being 'effective' means adopting behaviour which is correct or adapted to the situation. In other words behaviour that is desirable in one context may be maladaptive in another and, therefore, ineffective (Reddin 1970).

In all these models there is provision for the style which favours building a broader basis of consent, frequent and wide reference to the opinion of others, the involvement of their creative talent, and as full a participation in decision making as practical considerations and the wishes of individuals permit. This style is variously expressed in the models mentioned in this chapter – namely System 4, position 9.9 on the grid and the effective manifestation of the integrated category which is called 'executive style'. This seems to be the cultural adaptation likely to develop still further in the years ahead. It is now being argued that for management at large '... every scenario for business ... shows an increase in the autonomy of people at work, a trend towards consultation, participation, some measure of increased individual involvement' (Foy 1978:122).

In the case of education in particular it has been concluded that the schools which are generally held to be successful organizations are those in which management involves and stresses consultation, team work and participation. The procedures necessary for this to happen are not concerned to produce *uniformity* but to achieve *unity*. If some members of staff still have reservations about policies and practices which have received substantial support from their colleagues, they rarely withhold active cooperation. Heads recognize that although they are legally accountable for the good order and effectiveness of the school's administration, power-sharing is the best basis for longer term development. The *kind* of leadership given by the head, therefore, is the most important single factor (Department of Education and Science 1977:1979).

However, care should be taken to ensure that the essential purposes of the school as an organization are continually borne in mind. Excessive organization maintenance costs are anathema to the realization of the objectives which any organization sets for itself. Hierarchical structures and directive management are economical in this regard but may engender frustration, low morale and disengagement. Participative structures and permissive management incur larger organization maintenance costs but raise morale and effort. Clearly, the beginning of administrative wisdom is to recognize that there is no single and certain way to manage an organization well. Variable circumstances and needs require variable

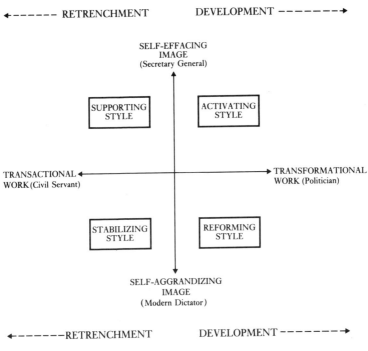

Figure 5.5 Variable management style model

approaches and answers. The manager must constantly exercise judgement about management strategy, and the degree and direction of changes in strategy which are necessary.

Modelling like this produces analytical categories which tend to imply strict alternatives, whereas in real life many individuals vary their style according to circumstances – though it is true that people representing the pure stereotype in any analytical category can surely be found. A good manager can vary his or her style as a function of professional skill to meet the inevitably changing needs of the organization. A model of this is presented as Figure 5.5.

In this model, organization at any particular time is positioned on a continuum from *retrenchment*, or the assimilation and consolidation of changes and innovation to *development* or the introduction and implementation of further changes and innovation. The number and scale of the changes and innovations determines the position on the continuum.

People in management positions at times of retrenchment move more into *transactional work* – the establishment and maintenance of new routines and the need to keep things going. People in management positions at times of development move more into *transformational work* – finding out how to get something going and making it work for the first time. These two extremes of the work content (horizontal) dimension can be exemplified respectively by the historic stereotypes of the civil servant and politician.

The contrasting dimension (vertical) is psychological. An individual concerned can display at one extreme a *self-effacing image*, leading from behind and gently releasing the creative energy of others, or can establish a self-aggrandizing image, leading from the front and commanding the creative energy of others. These two postures at the extreme are respectively exemplified in the stereotype Secretary General of the United Nations and the contemporary dictator. Since the point about management style is the effect it has on others, in this model the combination of self-effacing image with transactional work may be characterized as a *supporting style*, and with transformational work as an *activating style*. The combination of self-aggrandizing image with transactional work may be characterized as a *stabilizing style* and with transformational work as a *reforming style*. The upper half of the model is called *management by profession* to reflect the more detached nature of the styles exhibited, the lower half being called *management by possession* to reflect styles which exhibit a strong personal identification with the events of the organization. It is possible for the same individual to vary his or her style to match the varying needs of the organization.

6   Staff performance and development

The school as an organization is labour intensive. Its products substantially depend on the quality of its staff and on having enough staff. At the same time poor staff management is wasteful of staff or fails to make the best use of staff either in respect of their manifest capabilities or their potential. The staffing factor however is not merely a matter of the calibre of individual members of staff but of the way in which the work of staff is coordinated to produce a synergistic effect. Over a period of time staff members need the chance to be up-dated and to improve their qualifications to remain adaptive. The two important aspects relating to staff are, therefore, performance and development.

Job satisfaction

Most people at work like to know how well they are doing in the job. Some may camouflage this desire but the vast majority of people at work want to do a good job and to be known for doing a good job. Above all, they want that good job to be recognized by those who are in a position to know that a good job is being performed. In normal circumstances only a small minority may be guilty of indifference, cynicism or perverse ill-doing – pathological conditions arising from prolonged previous failure and disappointment, stress or vexatious local relationships which cannot be assuaged. Teachers in particular find their working day to be an unpleasant experience if they do a bad job. Most are not content merely to contain the job but aspire to competency within it, in the sense of this word being used in the national and institutional preparations for achieving competency standards throughout all private and public sector organizations during the coming decade. From the management point of view the concept of *job satisfaction* is worth keeping firmly to the fore. If a manager can help to increase job satisfaction levels in any way it creates a new asset for the school and almost by definition the greater effectiveness of the school. To achieve this result a number of basic considerations need to be observed.

The overall quantity of work undertaken by an individual in practice needs to be seen as a different quantity from that to which he or she is formally assigned. The two should bear a reasonable relationship to one another but owing to the great variability of individual staff they frequently do not. Seemingly equal assignments given to several staff will certainly involve differing workloads in the preparation and actual discharge. Some are said to be more 'conscientious' than others. Levels of intelligence and application vary. In this way overwork can arise from either the assignment side or the response side in the case of a particular individual and may affect his or her level of job satisfaction. Quantity of work viewed in this way is important for the individual since it governs the time available for home life and off-the-job activities.

The total work content for each individual needs to include some elements which are challenging and require special effort but lie within the scope of his or her potential. Exclusively repetitious work leads to stagnation and boredom. Too much novel work leads to stress and failure. In between lies the possibility for continuing interest in the job with advancing responsibilities and gentle growth. The *balance of stimulation* is the vital factor, varying as it does from one person to another. The recognition of performance is an important responsibility of management. It may range from the spoken word of thanks or praise to bestowed rewards such as increased salary and promotion for sustained performance over long periods.

Whilst the manager works to *increase* job satisfaction among staff members, he or she at the same time works to *decrease job dissatisfaction*. Job dissatisfaction and job satisfaction may be regarded as being on different continua, not the same one. A person at work thereby may be said to have a certain level of job satisfaction and separately a certain level of job dissatisfaction, each being based on different considerations. If job satisfaction depends upon having a stimulating work content, recognition, achievement, responsibility and advancement, job dissatisfaction may be said to relate more to the contextual factors within which they occur. These are primarily the physical conditions of the workplace, salary levels, the competence levels of the administration, personal relationships with colleagues at work, and, perhaps above all, the kind and level of management exercised, with particular respect to supervision.

People generally like to be thought responsible and need to have clearly delineated areas of responsibility within which they can exercise autonomy. However regulated this area of autonomy might be to take account of the particular individual's capability, mistakes are made and have to be tolerated. Different ways of doing things from those which a superior might favour also appear and have to be tolerated. Otherwise it is not autonomy. The mistakes and choice of doing things differently are a function of learning and growth. Too strict a supervision in this regard is almost certain to raise job dissatisfaction levels. The irony is that where autonomy is presumed by the superordinate, the subordinate so often seeks approval and reassurance before acting – either out of fear of disapprobation or from his or her own feelings of insecurity and lack of confidence. The superordinate may unwittingly create such insecurity and when approaches are made may be tempted into stamping his or her own methods and solution on the matters at stake rather than insist that the individual exercises the autonomy granted.

Performance assessment

The basis for reckoning the performance of a staff member is not easy to identify and define. Yet this is no excuse for not expecting to be called to account for one's professional performance nor to be reluctant to undertake such a performance review. In teaching there are indeed many subjective factors but this is also true of so many other occupations. One can search in vain for incontrovertible criteria and methods of assessment. In the end it is a matter of doing the best possible job at the time and improving the assessment system all the time.

Some elements which enter into the reckoning are quantifiable, such as punctuality and absence, pupil or student examination achievements under the National Curriculum or external examination system, and individual financial management under the school's budget. But for the most part performance assessment relies upon the perceptions and considered judgements of others with quantifiable data taken into account. A rule-of-thumb framework for assessing professional performance consists of five sections, as follows.

- Teaching mode and content
- Classroom management
- Business management
- Contribution to school life
- Interpersonal relations

Of all five sections interpersonal relations is the one relatively unfettered chance for the individual to present himself or herself to pupils, students, colleagues, parents, governors and others connected with the school simply as a person aside from the technical claims of the job. One can be a nice person to know even if a hopeless teacher. The reverse can also be the case. But the other four sections depend to some extent on the policy of the school and the professional and practical values and conduct of the head or other senior members of staff. All five sections are relative in the sense that an individual member of staff can be seen to fall above or below the average performance of the staff of the school in general. This could

	Assessment or appraisal by			
	Self	Subordinate	Peer	Superordinate
Teaching mode and content				
Classroom management				
Business management				
Contribution to school life				
Interpersonal relations				

Figure 6.1 Sources of data for a complete assessment of a staff member's performance

be starkly seen for example in a teacher's sluggish response over business matters, failing to carry out an instruction, ignoring a standing order or 'creating a scene'.

In view of the collegial nature of so many school staffrooms, attempts are made to derive a performance assessment from the perceptions and information supplied by a wider reference group rather than those of a superordinate only. Teachers have always been subject to the informal assessment of their peers and undoubtedly to the undercover assessment of their pupils and students. Assessment has also occurred for purposes of probation and changing jobs, though this is often less rigorous than it could be. The most energetic and thorough assessment ought to be that of self-assessment, carried out by the teacher on his or her own work. A full picture of a member of staff's performance needs data from several kinds of source, as presented in the matrix shown as Figure 6.1.

Although performance assessment is highly subjective in nature, it is still possible to have some firm points of reference to help to introduce more objectivity. One way for this to be done is to see that *positive standards* are set. These refer to what is wanted by way of performance requiring that a set of clear targets of achievement are established for a given job holder. *Negative standards* refer to what is not wanted, requiring the establishment of a maximum area of discretionary action for a given job holder. *Zero standards* refer to what must not happen at all, requiring the establishment of a minimum area of total constraint for a given job holder.

In assessing subsequent staff performance against *contributory standards* one is looking at the specific contribution of a given job holder to the overall objectives of the sub-group of which he or she is a member, or the school as a whole. This puts an emphasis on team spirit, sense of responsibility and accountability. *Historical standards* refer to the continuation or modification of existing standards, emphasizing pride in the job, reliability and self-justification. *Comparative standards* are those set by reference to performance elsewhere – such as rival schools – emphasizing competition, market appeal and wider awareness of conditions within which the school seeks to survive and prosper.

With the attempt to establish a legal basis for staff-appraisal and the undoubted advance into the design and use of more sophisticated staff-appraisal schemes – particularly in schools with large staffs – many questions involving rights and obligations arise, governing the actions of both those who are appraised and those who appraise. What is a right and what is an obligation, and for whom, are inevitably controversial questions. Table 6.1, therefore, suggests the ownership of what some of such rights and obligations might be. It is of course the qualitative aspects of a member of staff's performance in the job which matter most, more than the number of tasks undertaken and willingness to do more. To assess quality is a difficult part of staff management, but the guiding principle is that an individual should be effective in action. The assessment of this might take into account the following factors.

In the first place a person needs to have ideas. These may be primarily needed for teaching itself but with increasing seniority and advancement they are needed for the wider life and policies of the school. They need to be clearly formulated and communicated – either verbally or on paper in a lucid and persuasive manner and handled as such either in a one-to-one encounter or in a larger meeting. Those who are full of ideas however are not always able to test the feasibility of their own ideas. In other words, people can have wild and unrealistic ideas, which are as unhelpful as having no ideas. The ability and habit cultivated for subjecting one's own ideas to feasibility testing is a second stage of competence and attainment. The next element to look for is the individual's commitment to his or her own ideas, often called enthusiasm but which needs to be directed to oneself. After all, there are plenty of people in all organizations who can generate good ideas which are also feasible but are directed towards others. The hardest stages still lie ahead.

The next element is the ability to take practical steps. This involves extra work or different work to turn ideas into practical reality. It is a critical stage to be able to undertake because it raises risks for the ego and risks rousing the indifference or hostility of others. The next element in qualitative assessment of staff performance may then be the ability to overcome obstacles in translating an idea into practice, be they financial, interpersonal or technical. Beyond this again lie the skill and determination to see the idea through to full implementation and newly woven into the fabric of classroom or school life as an accommodated change. And, finally, there is the need to be able to maintain, develop and evaluate such changes. The excitement of innovation gives way to the requirement

Table 6.1 Suggested rights and obligations and their ownership in staff-appraisal systems

Rights	
Appraisee (employee)	*Appraiser* (employer)
to have a clear job description	to assume the individual knows what is required of him or her
to decide the ownership and use of written records	to hold any written records which are to be kept
to be enabled to make a different contribution to the school	to renegotiate the individual's contribution to the school
to be appraised	to provide appraisal
to be listened to	to reach and record conclusions on performance
to be enabled to grow in the job	to provide reasonable and proportionate means for the professional development of the individual
to receive adequate warning and be subject to proper arrangements	to make written records for future reference
to give reasoned explanations and be able to reply	to be frank on paper or in interview
to have individually negotiated minimum performance standards	to expect minimum performance standards to be reached
to have every help and encouragement to do the job as expected	to receive value for money

Obligations	
Appraisee (employee)	*Appraiser* (employer)
to account for one's own performance	to provide a non-threatening performance review procedure
to accept the authenticity of agreed reports and records	to provide security for written records
to accept responsibility towards the organization	to take corrective action with the structure to improve overall organizational performance
to cooperate in appraisal schemes	to have an effective appraisal scheme
to make the best use of time available in appraisal interviews	to give undivided attention
to expect proportionate consideration and opportunities which are fair to colleagues	to offer the individual developmental opportunities
to give adequate attention to the preparation of documents and interviews	to review records fully in preparation for interviews
to be objective and non-abusive	to be receptive and accommodating
to have understood the required minimum performance standards	to make clear what the minimum performance standards are
to make genuine efforts to reach minimum performance standards	to recognize and reward the attainment of required performance

of being able to iron out the difficulties in operating conditions and to perfect the idea(s) as a practical, operating scheme with proof that the intended results are being obtained.

The seven elements suggested form a logical and psychological sequence for carrying thought and talk into operational reality. In practice they are not discrete entities but overlap one another together offering a basis for checking through the quality of staff performance in something of a systematic way. No-one can be expected to be equally good at every stage but limited and one-sided performance can be identified so that steps for improvement can be taken. Some organizations are littered with aborted, ill-devised, neglected or poorly implemented schemes.

Development opportunities

At times of high staff turnover and plenty of openings for promotion elsewhere staff can determine the pace and direction of their own professional growth to a large extent. In times of stable staffing, management is obliged to be more active in maintaining and improving performance levels. All options enabling management to do this fall within a framework with eight dimensions, in four pairs. The first pair concerns location of opportunities which are either *internally* or *externally* available. The second pair concerns conditions which are either *voluntarily* or *compulsorily* taken up. The third pair concerns the content or nature of the opportunities, which are either for *up-dating subject content and method for teaching purposes*, or for the *development of management knowledge and expertise*. The fourth pair concerns the mode of developmental training which can be either *instruction-based* or *experience-based.*

Of the possible combinations in this framework, the one with perhaps the most potential, having been so little used in proportion to that potential, is that of internally available opportunity on a compulsory basis, followed by internally available opportunity on a voluntary basis. These two assume greater significance with the exercise of local financial management and the right to opt out of local education authority control. Development opportunities so offered amount to a programme of new investment for the school in parallel to that which must take place in agriculture, manufacturing and commerce to obtain more efficient technology from a combination of machine and method.

Three important means for providing internal development opportunities are job rotation, action research and project management. *Job rotation* is the opportunity for an individual to change jobs as a whole or in part with a colleague for an agreed period of time that is sufficient to gain knowledge and competence which otherwise would not occur. If the external dimension is brought into play, staff can exchange with colleagues from other schools or employment other than teaching. There are difficulties in job rotation. Reduced performance by the two people concerned may have to be carried in the interim but this may be regarded as the cost of the better performance given by the staff concerned subsequent to the exchange, not least involving mental refreshment as well as new knowledge and skills.

Action research is rooted in the assumption of responsibility for one's own problems and this extends in the school's case to having a more scientific attitude towards seeking solutions to problems by way of systematic investigation, observation, analysis and reporting as a basis for corrective action or innovation. The stage is now set for schools in future, given greater autonomy than ever before, to think of action research as a regular discipline built into the fabric of their management. *Project management* refers to the assignment of a defined task to an individual or small group to be accomplished within a given time-frame. It may be school-wide or external to the school on its behalf. The important feature is the need to allow freedom to the individual or group concerned to be able to design and implement a course of action to fulfil the objectives within the time-frame, subject to accountability for the outcome or results achieved.

> Three ways of offering staff internal opportunities for the development of managerial capabilities are
> * Job rotation
> * Action research
> * Project management

Basics in management training opportunities

Teachers who have any kind of responsibility for the professional work of a colleague need to be able to assess professional performance and to have some understanding of ways and means for inducing professional development. This is particularly true of staff who are concerned with the design, conduct, content and evaluation of training courses run by the school itself for its own staff as part of a staff development programme. Some staff also take part either as contributors or organizers in management training courses provided by higher education institutions or local education authorities. In all cases those who are subject to training opportunities, whether required or voluntary need to be able to select from what is on offer and to evaluate their experience of it in practice. The remainder of this chapter is offered for the consideration of all those inside and outside the school who have an interest as provider or consumer in securing effective management training for teachers.

A variety of *ad hoc*, short courses and substantial award-bearing courses may be offered by a wide range of bodies, including private organizations, local education authorities, colleges, polytechnics and universities. The assumptions of both those who offer such courses and those who become members of them are important elements in the conduct of such courses and the benefits derived from them. Care needs to be taken over several of these in particular.

Most course members have been in their schools for sufficient time to have gathered considerable knowledge and experience of the managing ways and means within them. A foremost need is however to encourage and require a course member to look afresh, to look long and to look closely at what is already very familiar to them but almost certainly not fully examined. Assumptions can easily obscure substantial management principles. For example, course members can overlook that a particular individual's or sub-group's managerial competence or performance level can be distinguished from that of the school as a whole. The managerial performance of one person or group is part of the managerial environment of another person or group. The managerial performance of the one is not exonerated or justified by either a good or a bad performance of the other. Good management is getting exceptional results out of unexceptional resources, especially in unpropitious circumstances. It is simply a matter of seeing that there is extra merit in an individual's or group's performance if all that is going on around it is detrimental to it but still does not prevent successful performance.

Conversely, if the general managerial environment is good then extra liability may be attached to an individual or sub-group which turns in a deficient performance. Teaching staff commonly think of the management of their school as an indivisible whole rather than an organic entity with many parts, implying that individual and sub-group performance is inevitably and solely shaped and determined by the competence levels of others – notably the head and other senior staff. By the same token, when heads and senior staff complain about the lack of initiative and competence in their subordinates, they do so with the assumption that their own managerial conduct and competence are not contributory factors.

Training therefore needs to induce sharper observation, more penetrating analysis and reflection. The improvement of one's own managerial performance cannot take place without the last of these. One way to induce greater reflection is to give attention to unexamined assertions and assumptions, whether written or spoken – hence the value in particular of managerial presentations in front of peers. It may just be possible that a greater readiness to assert and assume may exist among teaching staff in schools than in other occupations since it happens that the nature of the job involves much working in isolation from peers who would otherwise question and challenge both the preparation and delivery of all organizational work. The following examples are from actual practice.

> 'The larger the organization the more leader-centred it will be.
> It is less possible for hierarchical leaders to show their qualities of
> concern in large organizations'

These statements suggest a lack of personal experience. Very small schools can be very much a one-man or one-woman show. The teaching of the concept of structure and the study of alternative structures are intended to show the concept of structure both conveys and secures values. The chosen management style of individuals within it needs to be in accord with intentions. (See Figure 4.10.)

> 'Everyone wants to share in the management of schools'

This unelaborated statement may reflect the writer's own desires but needs the qualification that further thought and observation could bring. At the minimal level, all teaching staff share the teaching load. Responsibilities and duties beyond teaching contact are not sought by everyone and are only undertaken reluctantly by some when asked to do so. It is sometimes difficult to recruit governors from parents, staff and the wider public. It is a matter of concern always to ensure that those who are most eager to share the management of schools are also the most eligible.

> 'Autocratic headship is inherently wrong'

This is a straight value judgement. There is no reference to results but presumably it implies that the results obtained are undesirable or that results cannot be obtained by it. The single royal road to effective management does not exist. This particular style may apply to particular circumstances and to particular people. Autocracy means absolute power of government but no school head can rule in this sense. The term is often confused with 'authoritarian' which refers more to the rather unpleasant manner in which power is exercised and could be more justifiably judged inherently wrong.

> 'The structure reflects a traditional pyramidal organization. It has a
> senior management team'

The existence of a senior management team appears to have no bearing on the description that the school has a traditional pyramidal organization.

It may even be interpreted that the senior management team helps to justify the description and may convey veiled criticism. Team management by any definition would be held to be at least a modification of strict hierarchy, so it does seem that an understanding of the concepts of hierarchy and team management is lacking.

> 'Changes in working patterns are never popular with the staff concerned'

This assertion received no qualification. Staff at work are often conservative in attitude it is true but it is equally true that in any staff there are schools of thought, so that as many may desire change as may oppose it. Cases exist for change which are so compelling and self-evident that action is demanded. Cases for change which are less obvious need to be presented to staff. Changes which are not popular may be those which are not convincing.

> 'Staff see the programme as being acceptable – just. Everyone is happy – just'

Following a description of the programme referred to, this is the conclusion of a teacher with responsibility for staff development. It was based on personal judgement resulting from observation and interpersonal contact. In the absence of written data which might permit a more systematic investigation of detail, there would seem to be little room to undertake the fine tuning which the programme appears to need in view of its having only marginal effectiveness.

> 'I feel that the second-year team has learnt a great deal from the curriculum change that has taken place'

The writer may be right. The team may have learnt how not to do things. Feeling can give a present picture but facts are needed to move forward. A manager needs precise and accurate information, which involves an effort to gather and marshal.

> 'We decided to introduce shared reading into three classes'

The management aspect was in question, yet the content supplied consisted of a lengthy description of the reading scheme employed and a justification for the project but nothing on the process by which the decision was produced or that by which it was implemented and developed.

> 'The implementation of this proposed scheme would also benefit
> from the creation of more inspectors, regional coordinators and
> advisory teachers'

This statement reflects the casual approach of so many teaching staff in
seeking solutions to problems. There was no mention of cost and no
consideration of the implications entailed.

> 'Theories are simply not used very much in the realm of practice'

People on management courses sometimes have closed ears. This statement ought to be true of defective theories or irrelevant theories but any
off-the-job training inevitably involves theory defined as stored experience
and analysis of practice properly described. Theory as such is the basis
for all action. A training course needs to tackle prejudice allegedly against
theory which may well be a cloak for resistance to self-criticism and the
painful need to change. Such defensiveness on the part of individuals or
even whole staff groups may be made manifest by the classic protest that
'we have always done it this way', or any of the following objections to a
disturbing idea.

That's not our problem.

Why change it – it's still working
    OK?

You're two years ahead of your
    time.

We're not ready for that.

It isn't in the budget.

Can't teach an old dog new tricks.

Top management would never go
    for it.

We'll be the laughing stock.

We did all right without it.

Let's shelve it for the time being.

Let's form a committee.

Has anyone else tried it?

Don't be ridiculous.

We tried that before.

It would cost too much.

That's beyond our responsibility.

It's too radical a change.

We don't have the time.

That will make other things
    obsolete.

We're too small for it.

Not practical for operating people.

The union will scream.

We've never done it before.

Let's get back to reality.

Effective management training

Substantial courses in management education and training, particularly
those which carried degree or other public awards, were launched and
developed during the 1970s and 1980s. Course techniques at first relied
on experience accumulated in other subject areas. It took time and

experimentation to discover that traditional techniques were not always suitable for management training courses. A singular technology for training in educational management had to be fashioned. One of the most important elements in this matter was the question of superordinate or employer support for the course member. Traditionally teachers had used their own discretion with regard to additional qualifications and training for themselves. This practice raised few difficulties as long as course time took place in private time and made no demands on the teacher's place of employment. But management training may require release time for the whole or part of the course and above all else may need to involve the teacher in observations and investigations within the school or other kinds of activity which require the support or perhaps the actual sponsorship of the head. Real problems may become subject to scrutiny. Furthermore, a teacher's further training in management is likely to be effective if the school can take the additional training into account when the training period has ended. This is not to imply that the voluntary aspect of taking up management training might be replaced by systematic required training. Voluntariness almost guarantees good motivation, whereas the routine exposure to management training courses in industry and commerce over the years has often led to undermotivation and, at worst, cynicism.

Given the voluntary aspect, then, it is important for the effectiveness of a course if the following three conditions exist.

1. The sympathy and support of each course member's own superordinate colleague(s).
2. The adoption of an investigative stance addressed primarily to the course member's own or related place of work and its management problems.
3. The reinforcement of motivation by using opportunities for cooperative work with fellow course members and the course member's own colleagues at work.

The course content itself, aimed at increasing a member's competence, needs to be dominated by three sets of considerations which are presented under the titles *Management perspective*, *Professional value* and *Technical skills*.

Management perspective.   If the course is in education management then its content must be strictly disciplined to the management perspective. Teachers can pass through such courses with a very unclear concept of management. Having been, as teachers, historians, musicians, artists, mathematicians, physicists, chemists, biologists or linguists, they may then continue to talk and write in those various capacities but not as managers.

It is essential from the outset for course members to begin to think and feel in managerial terms, which may be far from their customary ways of thinking and feeling in their teaching subjects but must be in addition to them.

Management concepts need to be introduced, discussed and thoroughly understood. This can be facilitated by a knowledge of some of the management literature at large, together with that from education in general and particular sector literature as necessary. Concepts and practices currently subject to research would need to be prominent as would the inevitable questions of performance criteria for individuals, managerial groups and whole schools. Of a number of fundamentals, the loss of the stable state needs to be brought early to the attention of course members. There is really no need to talk of the management of change as so often occurs, since change is inevitable and without it there is no need for management anyway. Change has to be interpreted broadly, its constant ebb and flow being created *internally* by the natural wastage of assets; the unwanted actions of organization members; innovation (deliberate intervention) by management; and *externally* by legal requirements and additions; the random effects of competition from rivals; the unwanted actions of others.

Professional value. The prime objective of an education management course needs to be the improvement of the professional management performance of the course member on return to his or her own school. Every opportunity which can be found to use the teacher's own school for course purposes would therefore seem to be justified. The school can provide the course member with raw material for presentations in group sessions and for written work. It most importantly needs to be the focus of any research dissertation or thesis. In this way the course can remain relevant and topical with a continuing emphasis on *emerging* problems in practice, although past problems – whether solved or unsolved – can have selective use as case study material. A premium needs to be placed at all times on investigation and the collection of data in the field, the discovery and study of examples of good practice, effective ideas and successful implementation. This prime objective can in part be served by cultivating the management education of a course member on a wider front but this need not be disembodied from his or her operational experience and should not be at the expense of relevance. The improvement of managerial performance abhors a vacuum. The 'transfer of learning' process may be too much left to chance. The wider field of management may be harvested for good use provided explicit connections are made, as illustrated by the following example from actual practice.

Question set by tutor for a teacher's coursework:
What contribution has Taylor made to organization theory?
Suggested alternative for the purposes of this chapter:
Indicate and account for the extent of Taylorite principles operating in your school.

It may be noted in this example that the question as set is not only detached from any application but presupposes exclusively desk work by way of response, that is, the traditional essay in prose. The suggested alternative compels an understanding of Taylor's theory and practice of scientific management but as a vehicle to the greater knowledge and understanding of school management.

The written word in award-bearing courses has always played a central part. Oral work in contrast has needed encouragement. Both dimensions are important for management training. Managerial work in schools depends primarily on the spoken word to maintain systems already in place and to implement new decisions. So much is conveyed by the spoken word accompanied by body language. Tone of voice and speed of speech are modifiable attributes which affect the willingness of others to listen and respond as desired. The contents of what is spoken needs to be governed by accuracy, brevity and clarity as in the written word and these are attributes which are trainable. Training courses can find ways and means to improve performance levels of teachers in public speaking, applying to a range of situations from the chairing of meetings to addressing large gatherings of parents. By the very nature of teaching work, teachers are usually verbally very able. Ability in the written word however gets little comparative practice in the course of teaching. Yet the demands of school management have increased the need for written materials of many kinds, including the preparation of curriculum content, position papers on policy, letters to all types of bodies outside the school, the advocacy of new departures, the minutes of meetings and instructions and guidelines for the actions of others. In this connection it is worth teaching the idea of a 'management paper' since so much writing by teachers reflects the verbal mode in being too verbose. A management paper also aims to be accurate, brief and clear, persuasive and with a logical structure, contained if at all possible on one side of A4. It needs a title and a statement of purpose or objective. Prose as such is abandoned in favour of a list of points, arguments or information in words and/or figures and/or diagrams, with a conclusion on what must be done and by what means.

The emphasis which needs to be made on such features as evidence, fieldwork, observation, data and research sometimes becomes misunderstood by course members who say they are looking for 'a body of management *teaching*', 'management principles' and 'management knowledge'. Some members are even looking for a 'quick fix' experience as if management were like a model kit which can be readily assembled once the parts are known.

The philosophy of a course probably needs to be made clear to prospective members before membership of it is contracted. The judicious timing of course content, events and requirements however can ensure a smooth transition of understanding for course members, many of whom may have had little previous experience of management ideas and practices.

Technical skills.   The necessary emphasis on skills really embodies the notion of the importance of applied, relative to inert, knowledge. In management what a person can do as a complex whole is more important than what he or she can say or write, although the instrumentality of both of these modes is self-evident. Skills have a wide range of meaning in the practice of management and this needs to be reflected in any management training course. Included are interpersonal, quantitative, written and mechanical skills. Obvious sub-categories include using hardware and software for administrative purposes, some facility with accounting and financial management, timetabling, preparing agendas and minutes, chairing meetings, addressing large gatherings, the ability to prepare a variety of public and managerial documents, the ability to interview and be interviewed, handling the media, parents and business people, undertaking staff appointments and appraisal, knowing the law, planning and forecasting. Less obvious but underlying everything which is done are the skills of analysis and synthesis, careful observation, argumentation, the ability to arrange data logically and having techniques for handling bodies of data. Both hard and soft data have a place in school management. The former is objective and impersonal in nature, now typified above all by financial data, the latter is subjective and humanistic in nature. Written course work can contribute to skills training very noticeably if care is exercised to brief course members fully and to enforce good standards. The following is a suggested ten-point check scheme.

1. Is there a title which corresponds to the content?
2. Is it dated, with the author's name and institution of origin?
3. Is there a clear statement of purpose, or the clear isolation of a problem or matter to be reviewed?
4. Is there a good structure, with headings, sub-headings and other suitable devices to aid the reader's understanding?
5. Is there quality rather than quantity, analysis rather than extended description?
6. Is the content presented in a variety of ways – by prose, tabulations, figures, diagrams, charts?

7. Are the data (evidence) marshalled and summarized competently?
8. Are conclusions drawn?
9. Are there recommendations for action?
10. Is the paper or document submitted in wholesome condition, with a
    high standard of presentation?

Written coursework must be expected to include some reference to antecedent work from the literature and inevitable legal and financial sources with or without documentary references. It should have a simple consistent and complete reference system within the text and linked to a bibliography. The content of such coursework needs to have a priority focus on real and emerging problems in practice where the cutting edge of development is manifest. The value of this content might be made subject to a variety of criteria, such as the following.

1. Would a stranger to school management know from this how you
    manage your current job?
2. Does it indicate in what ways your management may be deficient?
3. Is evidence for such deficiencies provided?
4. Are there proposals for changes in your management and how such
    changes might be accomplished?
5. What means are suggested for knowing that these changes when
    implemented have been effective?

In achieving the level of authenticity required for a management training course material is generated which must be subject to an appropriate level of confidentiality. This particularly applies to written work which contains sensitive material. Research dissertations or those deposited in libraries may need to have an embargo placed on them for a certain period or be made subject to limited access. Conversely, findings from coursework investigations and studies can be made available in digest form to those who have helped in producing them, such as colleagues as respondents or senior staff who have made data available. Other means of data collection such as video and audio tapes need similarly to be subject to embargo and indemnity.

Public awards in education management need to have as much validity and justification as in any other subject. With this in mind, some attention has been given to the idea of taking into account the teacher's actual managing performance in the real setting of his or her job – rather like the teaching practice which is incorporated into initial teaching qualifications. Some States in the USA have long since adopted such 'internships' as part of a qualification in school management. But it can become artificial if conducted in a school other than one's own, superficial in nature in being removed from internal politics and perhaps inevitably confined to a particular class of jobs. It is bound to be difficult to administer and validate and expensive to run. But the principle is surely right. The idea that an experienced teacher should submit an acutual project or defined management responsibility for scrutiny as part of a public award in education management has much appeal. Progress in using this idea of submitting a test piece in one way or another may become one of the main features in the field of management training in education in future.

Benefits of training

The direct evidence of benefit furnished by members of education management courses themselves can be split into three main kinds. They think first of the many human aspects of organization such as how to deal with difficult staff, staff development, communication, job satisfaction and stress. They think of the second category in terms of the technical aspects of organization such as interviewing, conducting meetings, organizational structure, management style, legal aspects and financial management. The third area is of the course itself, the benefits deriving from the interplay between course members and the relationships that are subsequently sustained beyond the duration of the course, discussions with tutors, visits to other schools, participating in structured discussions, leading a seminar and working on course projects with others. It is seldom that a course member claims to have received no benefits at all, although claims of benefit are not always in the direction of improved personal management performance but perhaps may be seen as having an indirect bearing on it. The following actual statements of benefit are assembled in four groups.

Group 1   The renewal of professional life
- it has got me back to study after many years and I have found this wholly beneficial
- the course has generated new reading habits and new areas of interest which seem to be persisting
- it has led me into searching for a new job, new responsibilities and has given me something to talk about in interviews
- it has started me studying again and I am enjoying it
- it has given me a new interest in teaching

Group 2   Increasing understanding of present job
- it has made me look at myself afresh, particularly in my personal relations with my staff
- I was looking for and found a conceptual framework for my job
- it has given me new perspectives on my job and new perceptions of and possibilities in the school structure

- being able to talk regularly with other senior staff, especially heads is very valuable
- it helps you to see the whole picture rather than the part
- it has made me much more aware of what is happening in group activity with pupils and staff

Group 3   Obtaining new knowledge and new skills
- I have learnt a lot more about problem-solving
- I find I can be more detached when tackling my problems
- it has helped me to know what to think about
- giving lead talks and presentations is good
- I have got a basis for further study and research
- it has been intellectually demanding and the work load has been demanding too
- it has given me new awarenesses over current practices, e.g. in handling meetings and in interpersonal relationships
- splitting into small discussion groups and then reporting back in plenary session is very useful
- the knowledge, ideas and skills will be put into practice
- it has opened my eyes to the new extent and importance of the law in schools

Group 4   Improving management performance
- some techniques we have picked up on the course I have actually tried out
- it has helped me to face up to the central problems of my school which I had begun to neglect
- there will be reorganization involving my institution and this gives me the chance to prepare for greater responsibilities as well as providing a useful qualification
- my study had led me to an understanding of policy which I didn't know about and made me consider how my present management and the programme I manage might be improved
- I have produced data and material which are of direct use to us in practice and, make no mistake about it, it will be used
- this degree does not just talk around management but actually involves the student's own professional work

In the years ahead education will continue to be the focus of attention and controversy. There is an increasing realization of the emerging asset value of education as nations struggle for survival and good order. The sharpness of international competition in manufacturing, commerce and the supply of goods and services of all kinds is bound to lead to a greater reliance on education, a proportionately greater investment in education and a more sustained scrutiny of what it produces. An expectation of competence prevails. The upshot is plain for all to see. Schools will be expected to have the best possible organization and management. Most schools are already well run but the momentum has begun for the slow but progressive drive for the marginal improvement of productivity. If there are no grounds for a radical shake-up of the organization and management in the case of most schools which are up and running well, there is a constant need for all school managements to cope with gradual change and to undertake the fine tuning necessary to obtain increases in performance. To achieve this as the school moves forward to even greater autonomy in future, all those involved – and particularly those with more senior management responsibilities – need to cultivate fully their interest in and practical application of the science and art of organization and management.

Suggestions for discussion, practical enquiry or implementation

1. Take note of the contributions made by different speakers at a meeting of governors or teaching staff in a school. Identify the characteristic ways of thinking about the school which they represent and discuss the degree of consistency or eclecticism which each shows.
2. Investigate how much time school governors, other than teacher governors, spend in school during the working day and how they spend it in the case of two contrasting secondary schools or two neighbouring primary and secondary schools.
3. Identify a major decision that has been made in any school to which you have access. Trace the process by which it came to be made, the circumstances which demanded it and the factors which produced the particular form which the final decision took.
4. Try out the problem-solving model when you next chair a meeting, using it to structure and direct the contributions of members.
5. Design and implement a job rotation programme for the staff you manage.
6. Find out the teaching staff turnover rates (teachers leaving and being or not being replaced) for the last five years in your school and discuss the findings with colleagues.
7. Follow the track and ultimate fate of an important document that comes into the school or is generated internally, using your findings to consider the school's management information system.
8. In the case of a school to which you have access, collect and classify as many examples of organization maintenance costs and organization defence costs as possible. Bear in mind that the elemental resources consist of time, money, space, equipment and materials.
9. Conduct a 10 per cent cost-cutting exercise for your class, department or school without loss of output.
10. Canvass colleagues for ways to reduce waste.
11. Carry out an audit for all the external bodies to which your school relates, classifying them in three sectors – professional, public/private organizations, and pressure/political groups – and reviewing

the school's relationship in each sector with a view to making improvements for marketing purposes.

12. With small groups of parents, pupils or staff, discuss and assign priority ratings to the 18 items of interpretative task statements shown in Table 2.1. One way of doing this is as follows. There are 45 points to be distributed among the 18 items. Begin by giving one point to each of the 18 items which you think is worthy of consideration. Of all the items with one point, some will seem of greater importance: give these each a second point. Of all those with two points, some will seem of greater importance: give these each a third point. Of those with three points, some will seem of greater importance: give any such items a fourth point. At least *one* item which has four points should then be given a fifth point. All 45 points must be used.

13. Devise a questionnaire for a study of the management style of heads of school or departmental heads according to the model in Figure 5.5.

14. Discuss with (a) a young teacher and (b) the head of the same school (or other senior member of staff) the way in which each thinks about his or her school as an organization and get each to depict the staff structure in diagrammatic form for comparison.

15. Survey your colleagues for their estimations of your school's position in terms of Figure 5.1.

16. Ask a range of teachers in each of two contrasting schools to rank in order the decision areas in Figure 5.3 according to their relative importance for the organization and condition of the school as a whole. Then ask them to identify the participation which they believe they have in each of these decision areas, using the three levels shown in the model. Compare the results for the two schools and discuss the implications of any differences revealed.

17. Find out how many teachers or departments have notified over- or under-spending on their budgets at the half-way stage of the financial year.

18. Carry out an audit of management projects that (a) have been introduced and (b) are going to be introduced. The audit should include a review of progress of each project for those under (a) and a consideration of timing necessary for those under (b).

19. Obtain and consider staff absentee records with a view to appraising stress levels in the school by comparing them with those for a similar neighbouring school.

20. Choose three contrasting subject departments in a secondary school to study how each regulates the content, quality, sequence and pace of learning in respect of the particular part of the curriculum for which it is responsible.

21. Review the physical attributes of your school for recommending improvements. It should include published rules, conduct governed by custom and use, signposting, traffic flows, and the state of safety and security.

22. Type – on one side of A4 in concentrated language – a summary of the school which is suitable as a preface for the school's brochure for marketing purposes, focused on its specific and unique competences and features with its routine and special achievements.

23. Analyse your school's published objectives in terms of their precision, clarity, timescale and attainability, and the extent to which they have been communicated and understood.

Bibliography

Alutto, J.A. and **Belasco, J.A.** (1972) A typology for participation in organisational decision making, *Administrative Science Quarterly*, 17(1), March, pp. 117–25.

Ardrey, R. (1972) *The Social Contract*, Fontana, London.

Argyris, C. (1960) *Understanding Organizational Behaviour*, Tavistock, London.

Ashby, E. (1966) *Technology and the Academics*, Macmillan, London.

Ashton, P. Kneen, P. and **Davies, F.** (1975) *Aims into Practice in the Primary School*, University of London Press, London.

Barnard, C.I. (1964) *The Functions of the Executive*, Harvard University Press, Cambridge, Massachusetts.

Bayles, E.E. (1966) *Pragmatism in Education*, Harper & Row, New York.

Beckman, R.C. (1963) *The Downwave: Surviving the Second Great Depression*, Pan Books, London.

Bernstein, B., Elvin, H.L. and **Peters, R.S.** (1966) Ritual in education, *Philosophical Transactions of the Royal Society of London*, Series B. 251(772), pp. 429–36.

Bidwell, C.E. (1965) The school as a formal organization, Ch. 23, pp. 971–1022 in March, J.G. (ed.), *Handbook of Organizations*, Rand McNally, Chicago.

Blake, R.R. and **Mouton, J.S.** (1978) *The New Managerial Grid*, Gulf, Houston.

Blau, P.M. (1956) *Bureaucracy in Modern Society*, Random House, New York.

Blau, P.M. and **Schoenherr, R.A.** (1971) *The Structure of Organization*, Basic Books, New York.

Bloom, B.S. (1980) The new direction in educational research: alterable variables, *Phi Delta Kappan*, 61(6), February, pp. 382–5.

Boulding, K.E. (1953) *The Organizational Revolution*, Harper & Row, New York.

Brodie, M. (1979) *Teachers – Reluctant Managers?*, Thames Valley Regional Management Centre, Slough.

Brooksbank, K. (1972) Management, organisation and discipline, Ch. I, pp. 9–12, in National Association of Schoolmasters (N.A.S.), Special Report, *Management, Organisation and Discipline*, N.A.S. Hemel Hempstead.

Butler, J.D. (1966) Idealism in Education, Harper and Row, New York.

Carfax Publishing Company (1991–) *School Organisation and Management Abstracts*, quarterly, Carfax Publishing Companay, Abingdon.

Chartered Institute of Public Finance Accountants (CIPFA) Local Government Training Board and Society of Educational Officers, (1990) *The L.M.S. Initiatives: Local Management in Schools – a Practical Guide*, CIPFA, London.

Clegg, Sir A. (1974) Much to worry us, The Times Educational Supplement, 11 October.

Coleman, J. (1966) *Equality of Educational Opportunity*, National Centre for Educational Statistics, Washington, DC.

Coleman, V. (1976) *Stress Control*, Eurostates Marketing, London.

Cooper, C. and **Marshall, J.** (1978) *Understanding Executive Stress*, Macmillan, London.

Croner Publications. (1991) *The Head's Legal Guide*, (quarterly updates), Croner Publications, Kingston upon Thames.

Dale, E. (1969) *Audio-Visual Methods in Teaching*, Holt, Rinehart and Winston, New York.

Department of Education and Science (1965) *Circular 10/65*, London.

Department of Education and Science (1970) *HMI Today and Tomorrow*, London.

Department of Education and Science (1977) *Ten Good Schools*, HMSO, London.

Department of Education and Science (1979) *Aspects of Secondary Education in England – A Survey by H.M. Inspectors of Schools*, HMSO, London.

Donaldson, P.R. (1970) *Role Expectations of Primary School Headteachers*, Unpublished Dissertation for the Diploma in Child Development, University of London.

Dreeben, R. (1973) The school as a workplace, Ch. 14. pp. 450–73, in Travers, R. (ed.), *Second Handbook of Research on Teaching*, Rand McNally, Chicago.

Dunham, J. (1979) *Organizational Stress in Schools*, unpublished paper, University of Bath.

Dunham, J. (1988) The pressures and coping strategies of primary school principals, *Oideas*, 32.

Dunham, J. (1989) *Stress in Teaching*, Routledge, London.

Dunham, J. (1990) *Your Changing Role in Teaching*, New Education Press, London.

Dunsire, A. (1979) *Administration – the Word and the Science*, Martin Robertson Oxford.

Emmet, D. (1967) *Rule, Roles and Relations*, Macmillan, London.

Etzioni, A. (1961) *A Comparative Analysis of Complex Organizations*, Free Press, Glencoe, Illinois.

Etzioni, A. (1964) *Modern Organizations*, Prentice Hall, Englewood Cliffs, New Jersey.

Fidler, B. and **Cooper, R.** (1988) *Staff Appraisal in Schools and Colleges*, Longman, Harlow.

Forward, R.W. (1971) *Teaching Together*, Themes in Education, No. 27, University of Exeter, Institute of Education, Exeter.

Foy, N. (1978) *The Missing Links: British Management Education in the Eighties*, Oxford Centre for Management Studies, Oxford.

Frankl, V.E. (1967) *Psychotherapy and Existentialism*, Simon and Schuster, New York.

Furlong, M. (1973) *The End of our Exploring*, Hodder and Stoughton, London.

Gagné, R.M. and **Briggs, L.J.** (1979) *Principles of Instructional Design*, Holt, Rinehart and Winston, New York.

Gouldner, A.W. (1955) *Patterns of Industrial Democracy*, Routledge and Kegan Paul, London.

Gray, H.L. (1979) *The School as an Organization*, Nafferton Books, Driffield.

Greenfield, T.B. (1977) When does self belong to the study of organizations: Response to a sympósium, *Educational Administration*, 6(1), Winter.

Halpin, A.W. (1966) *Theory and Research in Administration*, Macmillan, New York.

Handy, C.B. (1976) *Understanding Organizations*, Penguin, Harmondsworth.

Herzberg, F. (1966) *Work and the Nature of Man*, World Publishing Company, New York.

Hicks, H.G. (1972) *The Management of Organizations: A Systems and Human Resources Approach*, McGraw-Hill, New York.

Howells, G.W. (1972) *Executive Aspects of Man Management*, Pitman, London.

Hughes, M.G. (ed.) (1975) *Administering Education: International Challenge*, Athlone Press, London.

Hughes, M.G. (ed.) (1976) Barr Greenfield and organization theory: a symposium, *Educational Administration*, 5(I), Autumn, pp. 1–13.

Illich, I. (1973) *Deschooling Society*, Penguin, Harmondsworth.

International Labour Office (1964) (1978) *Introduction to Work Study*, Geneva.

Jackson, K. (1975) *The Art of Solving Problems*, Heinemann, London.

James, E. (1949) *An Essay on the Content of Education*, Harrap, London.

Jarman, C. (1977) A survival kit for children transferring to secondary school, *Where*, 124, January, pp. 4–5.

Jencks, C. *et al.* (1973) *Inequality: A Reassessment of the Effect of Family and Schooling in America*, Allen Lane, London.

Jennings, A. (1975) The participation of the teaching staff in decision-making in schools, pp. 24–40, in Andrews, P. and Parkes D. (eds) Participation, Accountability and Decision-Making at Institutional Level, *Proceedings of the Third Annual Conference of the British Education Administration Society*, Spring, British Educational Administration Society, Coombe Lodge, Blagdon, Bristol.

Kingdon, D.R. (1973) *Matrix Organization*, Tavistock, London.

Koerner, J.D. (1968) *Reform in Education: England and the United States*, Weidenfeld and Nicolson, New York.

Laing, R.D. (1967) *The Politics of Experience*, Penguin, Harmondsworth.

Lawson, W. (1957) Neo-Thomism, Ch. 2, pp. 43–59 in Judges, A.V. (ed.) *Education and the Philosophic Mind*, Harrap, London.

Light, A.J. (1973) Staff development in education – the search for a strategy, pp. 5–10 in Pratt, S. (ed.) *Staff Development in Education*, Councils and Education Press, London.

Likert, R. (1961) *New Patterns of Management*, McGraw-Hill, New York.

Likert, R. (1967) *The Human Organization: Its Management and Value*, McGraw-Hill, New York.

Lockyer, K.G. (1962) *Factory Management*, Pitman, London.

Lyons, T.P. (1971) *The Personnel Function in a Changing Environment*, Pitman, London.

McGregor, D. (1960) *The Human Side of Enterprise*, McGraw-Hill, New York.

McGregor, D. (1967) *The Professional Manager*, McGraw-Hill, New York.

Melhuish, A. (1978) *Executive Health*, Business Books, London.

Misumi, J. and Tasaki, T, (1965) A study of the effectiveness of supervisory patterns in a Japanese hierarchical organization, *Japanese Psychological Review*, 7(4), December, pp. 151–62.

Morris, V.C. (1961) *Philosophy and the American School*, Houghton Mifflin, Boston.

Morris, V.C. (1966) *Existentialism in Education*, Harper and Row, New York.

Nash, P., Kazamias, A.M. and Perkinson, H.J. (eds) (1967) *The Educated Man: Studies in the History of Educational Thought*, Wiley, New York.

National Association of Schoolmasters/Union of Women Teachers (NAS/UWT) (1976) *Stress in Schools*, (NAS/UWT) Hemel Hempstead.

Packwood, T. (1977) The school as a hierarchy, *Educational Administration*, 5(2), Spring, pp. 1–6.

Paisey, A. (ed.) (1990) Organisation and Management Section 4, in Entwistle, N. (ed.) *Handbook of Educational Ideas and Practices*, Routledge, London.

Paisey, A., and A. (1988) *Effective Management in Primary Schools*, Blackwell, Oxford.

Paisey, H.A.G. (1975) *The Behavioural Strategy of Teachers in Britain and the United States*, National Foundation for Educational Research, Slough.

Pellegrin, R.J. (1976) Schools as work settings, Ch. 8. pp. 343–74, in Dubin, R. (ed.) *Handbook of Work, Organization and Society*, Rand McNally, Chicago.

Peters, R.S. (1966) *Ethics and Education*, Allen and Unwin, London.

Popper, S.H. (1967) *The American Middle School: An Organizational Analysis*, Blaisdell, Waltham, Massachusetts.

Pugh, D.S. and Hickson, D.J. (1976) *Organizational Structure in Context: Aston Programme I*, Saxon House, London.

Reddin, W.J. (1970) *Managerial Effectiveness*, McGraw-Hill, New York.

Reuchlin, M. (1964) *Pupil Guidance, Facts and Problems*, Council for Cultural Cooperation of the Council of Europe, Strasbourg.

Riggs, F.W. (1957) Agraria and industria – towards a typology of comparative administration, in Giffin, W.J. (ed.) *Towards the Comparative Study of Public Administration*, Indiana University Press, Bloomington, Indiana.

Rutter, M. et al. (1979) *Fifteen Thousand Hours: Secondary Schools and their Effects on Children*, Harvard University Press, Cambridge, Massachusetts.

Schon, D. (1971) *Beyond the Stable State*, Temple Smith, London.

Sim, M. (1970) *Tutors and their Students*, Livingstone, London.

Simmons, D.D. (1971) Management styles, REA, 14–121, 1–4, in Simmons, D.D. (ed.) College Management – Readings and Cases, I, The Further Education Staff College, Coombe Lodge, Blagdon, Bristol.

Stinnett, T.M. (1968) Teacher professionalization: challenge and promise, **Part V**, pp. 352–9 in Havighurst, R.J. *et al.* (eds) *Society and Education*, Allyn and Bacon, Boston.

Taylor, B. (1975) Comparison between types of institution in an LEA, pp. 3–11, in Andrews, P. and Parkes, D. (eds.), Participation, accountability and decision-making at institutional level, *Proceedings of the Third Annual Conference of the British Education Administration Society*, Spring.

Taylor, F.W. (1947) *Scientific Management*, Harper and Row, London.

The Daily Telegraph (1979) Saturday, 19 May.

The Henley Standard (1979) Thursday, 14 December.

Thomas, S. (1980) What makes teachers tired?, *The Guardian*, Tuesday, 11 March.

Thompson, J.D. (1967) *Organizations in Action*, McGraw-Hill, New York.

Thornbury, R., Gillespie, J. and Wilkinson, G. (1979) *Resource Organization in Secondary Schools: Reports of an Investigation*, Council for Educational Technology, London.

Turner, C. (1977) Organizing educational institutions as anarchies, *Educational Administration*, 5(2) Spring, pp. 6–12.

Tyler, R.W. (1967) The knowledge explosion; implications for secondary education, in Full, H. (ed.), Part 2, pp. 106–14, *Controversy in American Education: An Anthology of Crucial Issues*, Macmillan, New York.

Urwick, L. (1963) *The Elements of Administration*, Pitman, London.

Walsh, D. (1979) Classroom stress and teacher burnout, *Phi Delta Kappan*, 61(4), December, p. 253.

Watts, A.G. (1974) Teaching decision making, *The Times Educational Supplement*, 8 March.

Watts, J. (1976) Sharing it out: the role of the head in participatory government, Ch. 7, pp. 127–36, in Peters, R.S. (ed.), *The Role of the Head*, Routledge and Kegan Paul, London.

Whan, L. (1988) 'It's Friday and I know it'! Observations of a principal at work, *Journal of Educational Administration*, 26(2), pp. 141–58.

Wheeler, G.E. (1971) Organisational stress, Commentary on the case study 'A Head of His Time', ORG 14–100(3), pp. 1–4, in Simmons, D.D. (ed.) *College Management – Readings and Cases*, I, The Further Education Staff College, Coombe Lodge, Blagdon, Bristol.

Wright, B. (1975) *Executive Ease and Disease*, Gower, London.

Wyant, T.G. (1971) *Systems Thinking*, unpublished, Coventry College of Technology.

Young, A. (1986) *The Manager's Handbook*, Sphere Reference, London.

Index